# THE PICK UP BIBLE WITH TIPS AND TRICKS [2 IN 1]

## How to Cheat Without Getting Caught

Lil Rey

This document is geared towards providing exact and reliable information in regards to the topic and issue covered. The publication is sold with the idea that the publisher is not required to render accounting, officially permitted, or otherwise, qualified services. If advice is necessary, legal or professional, a practiced individual in the profession should be ordered.

- From a Declaration of Principles which was accepted and approved equally by a Committee of the American Bar Association and a Committee of Publishers and Associations.

The information provided herein is stated to be truthful and consistent, in that any liability, in terms of inattention or otherwise, by any usage or abuse of any policies, processes, or directions contained within is the solitary and utter responsibility of the recipient reader. Under no circumstances will any legal responsibility or blame be held against the publisher for any reparation, damages, or monetary loss due to the information herein, either directly or indirectly.

Respective authors own all copyrights not held by the publisher.

The information herein is offered for informational purposes solely, and is universal as so. The presentation of the information is without contract or any type of guarantee assurance.

The trademarks that are used are without any consent, and the publication of the trademark is without permission or backing by the trademark owner. All trademarks and brands within this book are for clarifying purposes only and are the owned by the owners themselves, not affiliated with this document.

# Table of Contents

## HOW TO PICK UP ANYONE

# HOW TO PICK UP ANYONE

The Bullet Proof Program to Never Hear a NO and

Hypnotize Her in a Second

**Lil Rey**

# Table of Contents

# Introduction

BDSM includes a number of various sexual activities that may rely on one or two specific factors, including -B&D (bondage and discipline) -D&S (dominance and submission) -S&M (sadism and masochism) Practitioners pursue this through a range of different acts that seek either a physical reaction inside their mate, a psychological reaction or both.

A widespread myth is that all kink types of BDSM include incredibly traumatic inflictions. Also, anything as easy as dragging somebody's fingernails down the back or gentle spanking will come under the BDSM umbrella. Engagement rates in BDSM can vary from casual one-time experimenting to devoted adherents ascribing to it as a lifestyle, and everything in between.

Sometimes (but not always) BDSM entails one person taking on the position of "Dom(inant)" and directing the direction of events, while a counterpart plays the role of "Sub(missive)" and endures differing degrees of pain or other types of punishment at the Dom's side. (Some may often classify themselves as "switches," opting to behave as Dom or Sub based on the type of the situation).

Another widespread myth (widely perpetuated by movies and television) is that all Doms are relishing sadistic abuse of Subs with no concern towards their enjoyment. In reality, nearly all BDSM groups stringently emphasize the value of dialogue and agreement. A submissive is someone who receives gratification from being controlled and consents. Indeed the popular BDSM idea of "topping from below" includes an ostensible Sub regulating and exploiting the interaction whilst looking compliant and passive.Your body encounters a series of chemical shifts during the desire or limerence process of a partnership when the dopamine, adrenaline, and serotonin rates increase.

Your brain feels like a drug user's as you feel a normal high from falling in love. Your energy levels are increasing, and your need for sleep can wane as your attention revolves around your new interest in love.

You are anxious, eager, and blissful at the same moment. Love may be blind in its early phases when you subconsciously fill the blanks with optimistic data to complement the thrilling unknown. You don't notice the bad habits of your paramour, and your optimism is glowing.

After many months of blind affection, partners are typically moved into the process of partner or connection that is characterized by engagement, warmth, and protection.

This process is correlated with oxytocin and vasopressin hormones, which are believed to promote attachment and increase during sexual activity and physical intimacy.

Reigniting the fire in a partnership also requires action that reminds the brain and body of the lustful love process. Such practices can generate suspense, anticipation, and even anxiety but ultimately lead to chemical processes involving dopamine, adrenaline, and serotonin.

Only the happiest people can notice their anticipation and sexual appetite are diminishing with time, so keep reading this book on all the ways you can improve stuff in your sex life

# Chapter 1: Beginners guide to BDSM

BDSM may seem a fairly recent trend. The concept was invented first in 1969 as part of an article called "Fetishism and Sadomasochism," by Kinsey associate Paul Gebhard. But signs of such kinky actions extend further back in time. Most ancient civilizations portrayed sexual actions with characteristics of submissiveness or sadomasochism. Only the very first civilization had documented tales alluding to BDSM! Let's dive deeper into the ancient documents and archeological discoveries that indicate history is much steamer than you thought.

The first sophisticated culture in humankind was Mesopotamia, centered in and around modern-day Iraq. This goes back more than 12,000 years, where towns, literature, and the wheel were developed. Any of the very earliest stories ever published contain pornographic practices of conquest and humiliation, often involving a female goddess called Inanna.

Anne Nomis, an author of "The History & Arts of the Dominatrix," explains Mesopotamian cuneiform tablets portraying sexual fetishization in honor of Inanna (also identified as Ishtar), the dominant female goddess in the region. A goddess of fire, vitality, and battle, several stories include her entering the realms of other deities with a victory. Inanna bent back to her own sex. Through his humiliation, she compelled people to submit to her. While they sang for her, she whipped her subjects, tempting them into erotic madness. Another hymn to Inanna describes activities of crossdressing, altered state of mind, and "pain and pleasure imbued" practices.

## 1.1 What is kink?

Kink is a very common sexual activity in the minds of many men-one including chains, whips, and one person driving their spouse about. Even while consensual sharing of control and rough sex are a part of the kink interactions of many individuals, they are not the complete amount of kink. They should be very kinky and never go anywhere near a flogger or name anyone Master — so there's no reason for kinky people to wear leather or dress all in black.

Kink is often thought of as "a blanket word used to characterize a broad variety of sexual behaviors that are deemed unusual or unorthodox." What qualifies as "kinky" depends a lot on what the culture considers as "natural." Crossdressing and performing gender roles is sometimes deemed kinky in heteronormative settings, but this doesn't imply that any nonbinary is kinky. And as this comic about an asexual person joining a play party makes it plain, kink can be gentle, nice, and innocent at times. Kink can be whatever you want, so being kinky doesn't compel you to have sex or fulfill your fantasies in any specific way.

**Consensual kink**

"Casual kink" is much like every other form of casual activity at the most simple level: it is an interaction in which everybody is on board, content, and loving the entire time. But because kink can involve the exchange of power, role-play, and even exploring painful, challenging sensations, a consensual kink experience can look very different from how we envisage consensual vanilla sex.

Kinky people are exploring this tricky terrain by holding lengthy discussions around limits just before some play starts. That could take the form of a yes / no / maybe chart, where couples let each other know what sorts of things they are and are not in, or it might provide clear guidelines about what sorts of emotions or dirty talk are acceptable: "I like getting my nipples kissed but not pinched," or "You can call me Father, but I don't like being named Daddy."

## 1.2 Difference between Kink and Abuse

"Kink often helps anyone to put things to an end. It also offers us the chance to say no, and the other party should still accept that, "says Kae Burdo, alternate sexuality and partnership trainer located in Vermont. If you use your protected word and the scene persists with your friend, that's violent. If you don't encourage your spouse to set boundaries or disregard your wishes in spite of their own interests, that's violence too.

And due to some of the kink's specifics, certain stuff that might look totally good from the outside can actually feel like violence. Burdo states that people sometimes go into "subspace" during a sequence, a mentality Burdo claims is tantamount to being intoxicated or high. They are often more open to pressure when someone is in the subspace and less likely to make rational decisions about their own health and well-being — which ensures they are not able to renegotiate expectations or agree to something different. It might not sound like the big deal to alter the conditions of a scene when someone is in the headspace, but it can quickly transform a mutual, enjoyable encounter into one that seems disturbing and unsettling after the fact.

Kink can be thrilling, scary, physically draining, and often utterly daunting. But it should also be voluntary, and anyone who takes part in a kink encounter should still feel valued, protected, and inviolable because their limits are. It is not a kink without that regard; it is an assault. And being kinky doesn't make violence all right.

## 1.3 What Appeals BDSM?

There are few responses that are more convincing when it comes to explaining the how and why of sexual desire than "because it's in our DNA," or "because we're wired that way." From why people enjoy tits to why all spouses start scratching each sexual itch after seven years, we still accept a plausible-sounding biological reason for our sexual predilections – except, of course, when it comes to BDSM.

Many common kink psychological debate centers on unpicking early childhood stress, mental distress, or violence (as the narrator encountered in Fifty Shades of Grey). However, psychological excitement is not just about physical stimulation, and physical reactions are not confined to psychologically comfortable circumstances. But in the case of consensual kink, we could benefit greatly from more focus on the physical.

Simply stated, there is a science to spanking, to nipple torment, to candle waxing and to pretty much every other sexual act you might name where prolonging the sensation of contact or relaxation or safely controlling blood flow induces the release of neurotransmitters – such as dopamine, adrenaline or serotonin – that contribute to a chemical high. It's true that you have to consider that kind of physical stimulation to switch on, but if you do, having a person you find it attractive to position you over their

knees and stretch you in a way that encourages your body to release noradrenaline, adrenaline, and dopamine in anticipation of the spank, and then opioids on the point of contact are likely to be a pretty positive sexual activity

And it is being backed up by the study. Take, for example, those research by Queen's University's Meredith Chivers who find that vaginal blood flow in women engaging in BDSM is that as they watch kinky porn – about the same pace as it is for non-kinky women viewing vanilla porn. Conversely, when kinky women watch vanilla porn, blood flow does not rise, meaning that the brain has a part to play in regulating the blood flow and that people's brains who react to kinky stimulation light up the way those who respond to vanilla sex do. Kinksters' ongoing fMRI scans are likely to affirm what sexologists already hypothesize: nothing of kink-related attraction is neurologically or biologically abnormal.

Most of us have hallucinations and neuroses, have eaten fears, and some of us are working on them more than others and at various points in our lives. For a few, BDSM can be a way to convey such – while with many many, vanilla sex is. But most of us lack the necessary self-awareness to sort out the vagaries of our psychological motivations and sexual peccadilloes. If you and your wife step away from a sex act completely fulfilled and unscathed – or at least without permanent mental or physical wounds – maybe that's a result that doesn't need to be checked anymore.

## 1.4 Incorporate BDSM in your Relationship

When communicating with your partner about the idea of what BDSM is,

you might sound hesitant. You can be more specific with the sort of stuff you're concerned with, like spanking, scratching, or handcuffs. Now you are on the same page. When you bring into the bedroom various sex positions, the same holds true. Generally, you may like to tackle the issue while you are in the bedroom, and you can solve all your issues. It may include the public's understanding of what BDSM is or of your specific meetings. You Should not threaten or force your mate emotionally into BDSM.

One way to get your partner a little more responsive is to make your partner sound more enthusiastic about what you want to do. Arousal will lessen our responses to disgust and make our sexual thoughts more receptive.

You can still move ahead with the baby steps I prescribe. First of all, you should call for a spanking instead of playing with a leash. Maybe before putting on a full dominatrix outfit, you should add the boots only. Concerning constraints and blindfold, it may be difficult to implement them. Alternatively, think of sex if one of you is tied up, and then add a blindfold to one person, until the two are combined.

A reticent spouse will be confident if you realize that you can approach it to step by step in place of everything at once. Speaking to your partner about how you will always stay safe as you broaden boundaries will even help overcome your unwillingness to take part in BDSM. You will always ask that the two of you have a safe word to hold yourselves safe in a subsequent situation.

## 1.5 Safety Measures for BDSM

When you're a newbie at BDSM, take a peek at various styles of BDSM practice situations and acts you may be involved in doing. I highly suggest using one of these BDSM checklists that you can run over with your partner (or even yourself) and see what kinds of things are turning you on, feeling comfortable, and what kinds of stuff you're not totally in. The idea of doing so is that even though you're with a friend and they're talking about wanting you to do breast bondage, and you're confused about it, you're fully clear of what you're doing, completely no! And Yes! And yes!

## 1.6 Set Limits

Like establishing physical and emotional constraints in our non-sexual lives, setting limits in BDSM is also very necessary. We agree on both hard limits and soft limits in this style of play. While such boundaries are not fixed in stone and can shift when you get more familiar with playing, it is vital to have guidelines when you begin every BDSM experience so that both you and your partner know what's acceptable and what's off boundaries. It's also critical that you BOTH have these boundaries. For e.g., if in your partnership, the Dom completely refuses to bind you up and screw you in public, then this is a restriction that should be accepted by him/her. OR if, as a Slave, the Dom just needs to push you around with a leash on your hands and knees, even if you're not in it, they have to be good.

But how do you determine what boundaries are hard and soft? First off, it's important to know the difference between soft and hard as they hit limits.

They are well described here by Cassandra Carr:

"Soft limits: a boundary that is not firmly fixed in stone. It may be adjustable, it may be forced, or it may shift with time and/or through the practice or understanding of that form of play."

"Hard Limits: What anyone can definitely not do, typically non-negotiable (may or may not alter with time). Ok, the checklist I referred to above is the best problem, but for everybody, really, hard and soft limits are different! That's why it's important to look at all the different styles of play, and then the power is in YOUR hands to determine what you're doing or not going to do now, and maybe a year or ten down the line!

For the very same reason I mentioned earlier, Secure Words Safe words are incredibly valuable to have. You, Will, use the correct, safe word when you're in the moment when it seems like you shouldn't stop at that.

## 1.7 Use Safe Words

Safewords come in handy for a variety of reasons ... Perhaps you're new to this and think bondage sounds SUPER fun, but then you get into it, and for whatever reason (and I mean WHATEVER reason) you just don't feel it, you can use your previously agreed safe word and play can stop or be readjusted.

But how can you make sure phrases come up? A lot of BDSM plays continue with the traffic light method, "Yellow" means "slow down" or "I may start feeling awkward." If you want to quit absolutely and automatically, whether for pain, irritation, or some cause, then using "Red" is the thing to do. "Green" means, of course, "all is fine and so keep going."

It's necessary to have a word to tell everything is well because checking in is the Dom's main duty. Also, it is important that the Sub feel safe enough to communicate how they feel through the process.

These are fairly common terms, so you can use certain phrases. Personally, it can be any term that you are confident using, but I would strongly suggest avoiding utilizing terms that you might usually use in the bag, or phrases such as "no" or "stop" that may be part of the game.

We have had the toughest time with positive terms growing up. I didn't want to say something so spontaneous as "pickle" or "banana" because I was afraid that if I spontaneously screamed, "BANANA" in bed, I might break out laughing. We finished by choosing "slow" to mean "slow down," "pause," to mean "stop" and "golden" as in, "I'm golden" to say it's all right.

## 1.8 Keep an Eye

Check-in is a very necessary part of the game, especially the intense BDSM action. When a Dom or Top checks in, it implies they are wondering quite clearly how they feel about the play at the edge. This even suggests you have to say you're more than just perfect, from a bottom-up. Say the top whether you're fine or poor, whether there's anything going fuzzy if you don't want to flog any further. The connection is key to ensuring the top start to learn how to make the play interaction successful for all of you.

Check-ins may be as easy as telling the bottoms to recall their safe phrases or to inquire how they are, or whether all is all right. It is, of course, necessary to allow good use of check-ins (re not all the time). When a bottom gives nice, reliable data, that can help the top make better decisions for all of you.

Visual indicators are another thing to remember with tops and bottoms, respectively. Are you / your friend looking/feeling dizzy? Woe to the weak? In so much trouble? If you see/hear any of these symptoms, avoid playing immediately. The Submissive Guide advises getting any soft carbohydrates, such as fruit juice or anything off to the side, only in the event of this.

# Chapter 2: Understanding roles in D/S relationship

Hopefully, you would find a spouse who is involved in performing your counterpart position, but that's not always the case. While you cannot compel the urge to control in another human, by taking on the role, you will illustrate how dominant he would feel, so that he will make requests and conduct sexual acts with you.

You may notice that your partner is involved in taking on the dominant position but is concerned about harming you. For some couples, this is a significant stumbling block. Getting a safe term will really make all of you more at ease. If you realize why you are turned on by discomfort or obedience, you can also clarify how you feel about that. You should reassure him, for example, that while it may hurt, you don't feel it in a negative way. It's something that arouses you further.

Anyway, if you are really serious about submitting, your boyfriend or husband will need to be encouraged. In reality, if he is engaged in dominating you, he may not appreciate what you are doing in playing the counterpart. If this situation occurs, then you will have to clarify it to him.

If service is a major part, then you will discuss how satisfying him actually pleases you too.

## 2.1 How to Be Submissive

It is a very rewarding activity to serve a Dominant. Lots of submissive beginners are lost, however. They have no idea of the role they have to play. They are looking for some form of fixing to make them feel more whole. Yet becoming a sub is, in all fairness, a lot of effort, physically, emotionally, and sexually. How will they face the obstacle successfully? Let's remember what it really feels like to be a strong sub.

## What not to expect from a sub

To be clear, A sub is not a doormat. They have thoughts and desires and thus will not be acting apathetically or passively. Anyway, a real Dom would not want a doormat. They want someone who really wants to be owned. Being a sub does not consent to abuse, either. Unlike BDSM, there are no restrictions or safe words to the violence. If you're a sub, be really cautious not to just give anyone your submission. Real submission needs first to be won. There are many poor doms and even criminals that claim to be Doms.

## Defining sub

An agreeable, respectful individual who wants to give up power is the concept of a submissive. They want to be used and need to be supported. They are the secondary member in a partnership, and thus "sub" is often pronounced with a lower case whereas "Dom" is always capital. A submissive may play several specific positions, such as:

• Small Girl

• Property

• Assistant

• Puppy

• Masochist

They aspire in all ways to satisfy their Master, not only sexually. That implies they would have to sacrifice any of their own personal freedoms and interests.

Getting a gentle and calm temperament isn't unusual for a sub. They are conscientious, and when required, they embrace discipline. Subs strive at always treating themselves in a polite and humble manner, understanding that their actions are a clear reflection on their Dom.

## Difficulties faced by subs

Subs aren't perfect; sometimes, they can screw up. There's always the reality that stressors like full-time work and kids are involved in a 24/7 partnership. Taking on behavior improvement and helping someone else while you're fatigued and limited for resources may be challenging.

Even if not in the presence of their Dom, a test to many is obedient.

One difficulty subs have to face is to top from below. They might revolt a little at first, or attempt to overtly challenge the choices taken by Dom. The easiest and shortest answer They can give is, "Yeah, Daddy." Eventually, both of their lives are made so much simpler.

## Master submissiveness

A sub will also note they will make life easier for their Boss, not harder. At any given moment, considering proactively what the Dom wants, and satisfying that would offer him much pleasure.

Of course, one of the best ways a sub will do so is sexually, and therefore it is a must to agree to any required act under one's contract. They will always seek to follow laws to the best of their abilities, but they can take it willingly if compliance is required.

Wearing a leash, even a discreet one in public, can help to hold a sub in the mentality of slaves. They are property held by someone else and, as such, serve their Dom. This will allow a sub to take immense pride in their bodies' fitness and presentation. How they can do this is:

• Proper sleep

• Exercise frequently

• Follow a nutritious diet

• Dressing appropriately

• Have decent grooming and toiletries.

True obedience is not just a job; it's a way of life. Being a submissive ensures that they are kept to a higher level, so it's worth it. They'll get the supreme gift of full acceptance from a Dom.

## 2.2 How To Be Dominant In The Bedroom

"Dominant" is a term that is tossed around a lot in the BDSM community. Being a Dom may sound really appealing. Most of them are people who want to be sexually more powerful in bed, but even in their relationships, and also in life at large. Alas, there's a lot of virtual Doms out there. How can you guarantee you don't behave like one? Or what do you look for in a Dom if you're a submissive? Let's remember what having a genuine Dom actually entails.

## What a Dominant isn't

Let's begin by concentrating on some of the warning signs of a poor or a false dom. If they're more focused on what they receive than what they're offering, that's a big hint. The essence of a Dom can, of course, be very greedy, but they will also make sure that the sub is fulfilled not just mentally, but also physically and emotionally. Most modern Doms are latching onto the notion of being hooked anytime they can, right at the start of fresh ties. Yet the trust needs to be won much like every partnership. A false dom may say stuff like, "You're not really a sub," or, "XYZ will make a nice sub." If you're a sub, don't fall in for that. So if you're a Dom, don't do anything like that until the sub wants to be talked about like that. It can do significant emotional damage.

## What is a Dom?

A Dominant is a strong, significant individual who likes to be in control. They long for obedience and must be in control. They seem to be the "Alpha Male," so that's why "Dom" is often pronounced with capital while "sub" is often the lower case. A Dominant may play several specific positions, such as:

- Daddy
- Master
- Boss
- Owner
- Sadist

They seek to exert the power of all aspects, not only over their sexual subordination. That means they have their own personal lives in order. Having an obsessive-compulsive attitude isn't unique of a Dom. People take immense pride in their bodies' health, their houses, cars, and careers, believing all of these are reflected in them. The Dom takes responsibility for their sub's wellbeing and proper training, guidance, and discipline. The Dom also ensures a secure and healthy atmosphere in which its sub can conduct its duties in the Dom's operation.

**Challenges to being Dominant**

Doms aren't perfect; sometimes they'll screw up. They will also apologize without being vulnerable by acknowledging exactly what they have done wrong and what they are trying to correct it. Doms are not expected to lose their temper. They might get upset and crazy, but they will still seek to stay in charge. Another obstacle that a Dom may face is moving against the norms of being good and compassionate with women in society. They are supposed to be the "good person." Because of that, many people consider it is challenging to be assertive in sex. They will still feel bad to take, but a Dom has to note that subs want to be used and to be physically exploited. This doesn't mean a Dom can't offer in bed, but only being more assertive about that aspect of the partnership can help them achieve their position. Forms a Dom can achieve that are:

- Holding their sub down during sex

- Tying up their sub in bed, so they are restrained

- Telling their sub what to do sexually instead of asking

- Delaying their sub's orgasm to show they are in control of it

**How to be more dominant**

Dom's body language and voice should be Efficient and in charge. They can look at the part, as well. They don't have to be a Christian Grey, but they're supposed to be fit, have good hygiene, dress well, and not sloppy. Doms should have a good posture and stand tall above the sub, often making them sit or kneel beneath them. A Dom should always talk with trust and be clear. They wouldn't say, "Where do you want to dine? "I'm taking you out for dinner, they'd say. Select a spot. "One of the best things a Dom can do is order the sub to make a coffee for him. When we were vanilla, I would ask her, "Can you please make me a coffee? "Now I just order her to make me a cup of coffee, and this simple thing lits up her face with a smile.

**How does a Dom train a sub?**

It's a lot of effort to prepare a sub and not to be taken lightly. It is, therefore, a rather satisfying operation. When a Dom trains a sub, they shape it to be a stronger version of itself. Modification of the behavior is achieved by the maintenance of structure and order. Subs thrive on a fixed schedule, and a Dom can provide that with rules and protocols. The sub will have a journal so that the Dom will get in their head. In general, penalties are required to help direct and correct them. It requires relentless work, so when the sub is just what the Dom needs, it is a wonderful thing.

True Dominance is not a pure task, but a way of life. Being a Dominant means that they are held to a higher standard, but it's worth everything. They get the supreme favor of the eager submission of a sub.

## 2.3 Role-Playing

It's always been our understanding that role-playing can be a great way to convey our fantasies in the bedroom, and "spice stuff up."

During the first time, a partner sprung up a role-play situation on me by dressing up in a suit and behaving as an authoritative manager in the workplace, the intimacy that occurred became very thrilling (after I managed to avoid giggling).

Role-play is popular among BDSM practitioners because it usually centers around a certain amount of power-sharing in the fantasy sense. The overwhelming majority of RPPs concentrate on the overt inequality of power between participants.

You may wonder what kinds of positions are there if you are new to role-play.

## Professor / Student

Who did not have the crush of a professor at one stage? Coping with the vision is important, right?

A trainer may be incredibly thrilling to know compassionately and lovingly (or sternly and dominatingly!).

Such scenes may contain 'reading' and assignments but also concentrate on old-fashioned activities, including spanking, paddling, caning, and other types of physical discipline, and on uninformed students who are arrested and imprisoned.

Find a fashionable school uniform for all sub-companies, and violate these rules!

## Doctor / Patient

Clinical encounters between a doctor and a patient sometimes include a lot of uncertainty, anxiety, and concern that makes this style of play especially appealing to clinical enthusiasts.

Such scenes may include intrusive 'testing,' the playing of needles, enemas, etc.

Those in the BDSM society see medical fetishism as a particular form of an operation because special safety measures for the activities it includes are required. Make sure you have the critical details handled by a qualified expert.

I firmly recommend that you find a specific curriculum or laboratory in the near BDSM community that integrates these strategies, should you want to conduct a real-time analysis to integrate these items as scalpels, urethral activity or saline infusions.

Basic: don't do anything for which you are not eligible.

## Caregiver / Little

It's a title often assigned to scenes of role-playing in which the top behaves like a father, mum, older adult, nanny, or a child nanny who performs the part of the person who is caring for. We've all heard the word "Daddy," adult kids, right? This is a definition of this nature.

This usually includes age, which indicates that the bottom deeds are junior or the top deeds are older.

It is a widespread misconception that age player is allowed by pedophilia or incest, but that is not the case. The draw here is the loving nature of the caregiver's role and mental independence to return to an infantile mind.

These scenes can involve children-oriented objects, including diapers, pacifiers, animals stuffed, bedtime, spanking, or other types of embarrassment combined with sexy action.

## Kidnapper or Burglar / Victim

This can be an incredibly violent way to perform the role of aggression and consensus-based interpretation.

A mighty Dom acts as a kidnapper or thief, and his target is violently overcome.

Such a scene takes significant preparations for a safe and voluntary pull-out. Once you plunge in, you're going to want to do more work.

For some, abduction can become an unbelievably complicated multi-day dream, as abduction scenes are sometimes called. Several sex workers are often trained in fetish stimulation. It seems to be a fun holiday!

## Law Enforcer / Convict

Uniforms and restraints, ooh da! When you feel uncomfortable about the thought of violating the rule and disciplining it, it might be up to you to take custody.

For same-sex inmates that may be especially true because offenders are typically segregated by age.

The probing may be a great part of prison games. Masters, bind, and "torture" your impotent spouses to acknowledge the information that you look for! For imagination! And, as normal, be very vigilant.

## Owner / Pet

Meow member, woof woof meow! Woof woof meow! All the excitement is now a pet activity. Many people like to dress and adopt their characteristics as puppies, cats, ponies, and others.

It is convenient for them to be in this headspace, which enables them to indulge in more basic aspects or degrees of playfulness, which they would not otherwise be able to achieve. Domesticated animals, however, are still slight and easy to handle, perhaps a total turn-around for kinky styles.

The training focused on pets and procedures are core elements of this style of role play.

You can also make dog/cat/bunny ears, bag, collar, petal, and other equipment. You may want to do this.

## Boss / Employee

Although I don't suggest banging your actual Boss or employee, a smooth roleplay scene can be especially nice if you are in the nature of crossing the boundary between a personal and professional partnership.

This kind of game may include characters, tasks, punishments, etc.

"You stupid clerk! I instructed you to register these reports over an hour ago! Splashing will help keep you focused.

## Master of the House / Maid

A personal maid to cook and clean my apartment? A persona? Jesus Christ, pass it on! The teaching in Maid role play is particularly based on service.

Tops, lead your maid, and tell them how you want to see your room, and don't hesitate to warn you when you mess with it.

Yeah, and see if you can find the hot maid outfit of your friend, who will allow you to plunge in the fantasy. There are some pretty interesting options!

## Millionaire / "Commoner"

Many of the unlucky plaintiffs would love just being distracted and exploited by an immortal cash-rich relative.

It is undoubtedly the explanation why "Millionaire BDSM," one of the more popular kinds of kinky sexual goods, has been delivered by 50 Shades!

Millionaires will naturally buy luxurious appliances and gadgets of all types and take their unfortunate partners to the nicest restaurants. While you do not have the resources to do so, there's no benefit in pretending to have a nice dinner and a luxurious hotel once in a while.

If you're the Dom in that scenario, placing yourself in the headspace of a billionaire. If you had all the money in the country, how should she handle your dotting companion? What do you want to use in exchange for your hard-earned cash?

## Royalty / Servant

Sleeping Beauty Debate, perhaps because the notion of being swept away and abused by a sexy, beautiful prince is so familiar, is one of the most popular romantic classics of BDSM! Yeah, Disney did a brilliant job of kicking both of us in the ass, don't they?

Servitude, imperial worship, human enslavement, shame, and a host of other kinky themes can be used in this form of role-playing.

In this case, a royalty servant will "have no choice" whether or not to satisfy the total balance of power in the master/slave system.

You and your friend can digitally discuss any illusion or complexities in a romantic situation through role play.

Discover and play fun and do not forget to integrate exchange, safe word schemes, and aftercare, as often when supporting BDSM.

# Chapter 3: BDSM

The human body is capable of putting on an almost infinite range of poses and roles. Some of these positions are uncomfortable, hideous, or unacceptable for adoption for couples, but for a Controlled Elegance, slavegirl should be seductive, graceful, and as attractive as practicable, in bondage or out of bondage.

The following is a list of called poses and roles, as well as more general changes and explanations that will help Masters determine the posture they want their slavegirl to assume.

By the way, in modern life, we are not always acting like misogynistic scientists of the 1950s. Ok, not so much, anyhow. We don't take all of that literally (except for the health side notes). It's a game for play scenes and the bedroom where the usage of loaded words such as "slut" can be enjoyable and sexy (with the right individual agreement in the right way) ... much as the slavery itself is sexy and pleasant, but only if performed consensually in the right situation with the right party.

## 3.1 Deeply Intense Bondage Positions

### Classic Damsel

That role depicts the silver screen's iconic damsel-in-distress. In the usual version shown here, the elbows are bound behind the back to connect together, the wrists are bound, and the legs are linked both above and below the knees and at the ankles. Together, the elbows create a strenuous bind, and the back location of the shoulders pushes the subject into an

unconscious show of the bosom, thereby emphasizing the subject'sattractiveness.

However, the fact that the legs are too tightly joined together makes some physical contact very awkward, and this is called a respectful posture that is appropriate for the show, taunt, and punitive usage.

The version seen here includes a crotch strap and a drawn-tightened satin scarf gag. Chloe says: "I enjoy this pose because I think it makes my body beautiful. Getting elbows bound together allows my back arch and my chest to stand up, which is not exactly comfortable, but it looks really sexy to me, and I have never been able to wriggle out of an elbow-together bind because it just doesn't provide enough movement to make that feasible. I like this place too, as it lets me sound like a naive damsel in trouble who is

not in immediate danger of anything very bad happening to her – I sound like a sort of bondage-statuette while I'm bound up like this; I feel like I'm more apt to be respected than exploited.

### Box Tie (Arm position), Frogtie (Leg position)

The box tie is the basis of several bondage situations, but restraining in the way that the elbows-tied together but without creating pain, or blood pressure and nerve issues. Thus, it is ideal for positions that require a significant amount of time to bind, while elbow positions together can be restricted to those where the elbows can be attached last and easily untied.

The form so developed is a little less aesthetically appealing than the elbows-together tie to many viewers but is still useful for the vast number of variations it makes. The ropes that move through the upper arms and chest prohibit the subject from wriggling the wrists out of the bind at the small back; this wrist rope may be connected to a crotch rope if needed for greater immobility.

The position seen here blends the location of the bow tie arm with the location of the leg of the frogtie. Frogtie is the derogatory term for the most convenient position — the leg is entirely extended to the hip and bound just behind the hip and just above the ankle. This makes for great variety in posture and some versatility, thus keeping the slavegirl from attempting poses above her station — it's difficult to rise up or lift her head over a certain point, which can be a helpful aspect of this bond. A challenge of embarrassment may be established by offering the compensation or freeing the slavegirl if only she could hit a token put at her usual head level — a position that would be impossible even though she was quick enough to be able to get to the knee stage.

Nevertheless, the main usage of frogtie is obviously erotic. Despite the constraints enforced by the chain, the subject can broad open its legs and can thus be brought through any or every necessary orifice. As seen in the first example in the second row below, certain alternative poses can still be assumed by the topic (the image shows an effort to reproduce the CFM pose when tied). Using a belt or rope to protect the shoulders or other protective device makes it easier to build many further combinations. Chloe says: "In this pose, I look even more like a slavegirl than I did in Classic Damsel; the arm posture can be held for hours, and I like the idea that I will be kept bound up like this all night. It's not almost as awkward as the elbows-together connection somewhere, but it always lets me lift my neck, and it still looks elegant. Now that I am the RE Slavegirl, I spend a lot of time sitting, but I guess you can probably tell by my face that I really enjoy it! You should literally kneel together with your legs in this tie, but I always overlook that because this way, it looks more attractive. "

## Hogtie

The hogtie's most important aspect is the cord that connects the bound wrists to the bound ankles. It's this function that ensures the hogtie provides the slavegirl with full restraint from limited exertion on her captor's part, which goes some significant way to understand her enduring popularity, especially in Western Slavery. There are few ways to immobilize anyone with as little rope as the simple hogtie so easily. Only binding hands, wrists, and a short distance between them may be most crippling and completely inescapable if the ties are placed in such a manner that they become invisible to snoring paws.

The version seen here becomes much more strenuous, adding extra ropes around the knees and around the wrists, taking them almost to reaching backward. It may make it very painful for certain individuals to suck in air

(because the weight on the lungs and diaphragm can not be avoided) which also ensures that the hands are likely to become stiff earlier rather than later, and this version would be deemed advanced for pain rather than long-term storage.

Easily achieve the same task with hardware, either with handcuffs and leg-irons (one merely needs to cross the links connecting the wrists and ankles) or with links and bolts. This is called a hogshackle in this variety. There are also bondage accessories intended to keep the person in that role, and such things are commonly referred to as "hogties."

Mobility is typically restricted to the ability to roll forward, and likely from there the ability to level up into a bridge role, as seen in the picture. Generally speaking, the person feels it more relaxing to be able to move, because it relieves chest pressure. When the hogtie is pulled close enough, then certain questions will typically be refused too much versatility.

Aesthetically, it has the tremendous benefit of equally showcasing the soles of the feet and the face and thus can be called the slavery counterpart to "the look" so coveted by foot fetish lovers all over the world. Chloe Says: "Urgh, I hate these! I still want to convince people to use the cross-angle version because it's a lot more convenient for me, but I guess most people want to see the look more. When my knees are bound together, it's especially hard, and putting elbows-together is much harder! In this place, I still find it pretty hard to breathe (although other models don't have this problem), so I guess I might need further experience to make me better at it. "

**Balltie, plus Legs Up-Balltie variant**

There are several variations to the style of the simple balltie. The key distinction is that the feet are pulled up to the shoulders and forced with rope to stay there. The outlined variant uses a single band of canned rope at breast level; if not otherwise protected, this could be vulnerable to any slippage. Many versions often carry the ties around the hands, use the limbs to prevent slippage.

Typically the balltie begins by connecting the wrists and ankles. For the standard version, both will be linked together (as here) would instead utilize extra rope to draw the binding ankles towards the body and hold the knees bent, either by stretching the chest band and loop and cinch across the bent knees and shins or by inserting a rope to drag the ankles for, e.g., to a crotch rope.

Alternatively, in this case, the wrists of the subject are tied to her ankles, but are not otherwise attached to the rest of the balltie, enabling her to take the pose of JBJS, or, as in the last two pictures, to be tied to her ankles elevated to provide the version of the legs-up balltie.

## Bent Over Bondage Position

Want to test your balance and flexibility? Try holding a <u>bent-over position</u> during sex or kink. This can be either a wide stance, like downward-facing dog, or a narrow stance with your hands near your feet. Either way, you might need your partners help to keep you up. But since hands tightly gripping your hips are part of the fun, getting an assist shouldn't be a problem.

Using a <u>spreader bar</u> is a simple and effective way to bind someone for this pose.

## Chair Bondage pose

Remembering the iconic Betty Page popularized "damsel in trouble," chair bondage is a beautiful entry-level bondage sex role. The place is simple to hold since the attached person is seated. When you have bondage furniture or a changed chair with a hole in the back, it will restrict sexual exposure, but there is always plenty of fun to have without genitalia. The role may function for oral sex, or for a number of kink types. This can also go along with more moderate sensation play as an entry-level position, offering a complete kink experience that is also amicable to newcomers.

A traditional type of chair bondage is literally wrists bound to a chair's arms and ankles bound to a chair's legs, but it often lends itself to a number of other configurations-the limit is your imagination.

Attempt some with basic bondage rope or bind your partner use wrist and ankle cuffs for this job.

## Armbinder Gag Bondage

Position Holding the arms behind the back provides immediate flexibility and is often harder on the knees than getting the hands bound at the foot. The role of the Arm bind Gag is great as it doesn't need a lot of versatility, but it also takes power away. A nice option is to apply a gag to the pose if you use string, which may be applied separately if you use other bondage types.

A gag may be a thrilling experience since it is extremely intimate to fill someone's mouth. It brings drool to the mix as well, which could be part of the fun.

Not even when you gag someone to provide nonverbal safe words in case the attached person wants to quit playing.

**Leapfrog bondage position**

Flexible feeling? The location of Leapfrog is simple to get into and provides multiple entry choices. When somebody's hands and ankles are tied together, you can also flip them over when playing and spice it up.

You may select whether to get the wrists inside or outside the knees, for still further choices. It may change the role experience, and the bodies of certain individuals may have a harder time for one or the other.

Use an adjustable spreader bar in this place for a simple way to bind anyone.

**Shrimp or Forced Bow Slavery Location**

The location of the Shrimp or Forced Bow is close to that of the Hogtie, although it is easier to sustain than it seems. Shaped as a place of punishment, being bent over inhibits ventilation, so always checking in on the constrained companion and making sure you let them out until they're too distressed or too out of breath is essential.

One of the helpful aspects of this place is that when they are sitting up, you can secure them, and then tip them over to reach their butt and genitals. This is more sex-friendly than a Hogtie as this place gets the legs out of the way.

For this place, consider bondage wire. Or use an armbinder and attach straps to the neck and ankle.

## Mummification bondage role

Mummification is usually a full-bodied type of bondage, so this is one where the restriction is the point of action, rather than sexual exposure bondage. Probably the most intense type of slavery, until doing this, it's crucial to know how someone responds to restriction. Even seasoned players will start to panic from tip to toe while they're encased.

It is this intense nature that makes Mummification attractive to certain kinksters, particularly those who want to test their boundaries. Customize the mummification encounter with plastic film, duct tape, pet wire, chain, or even full-body leather casings.

You can leave gaps or cut openings (using safety shears) around genitals or breasts if you choose to attach sex to your mummification games. This style of bondage is especially good for taunt and denial, or forced orgasm.

No matter what place you seek, note that sex and kink play is about the emotional relationship. Do not enable the dynamics to overpower the connection and ensure that you connect before, after, and after playing to ensure that everyone meets their needs.

## The Kinky Missionary

"The female on the other end is flat on her back, hands overhead and cuffed," says Carol Queen, Ph.D., Good Vibrations staff sexologist.

"You might even up the ante for the second set of cuffs around the ankles because the bed has legs to tie the cuff chain or a piece of rope on. The dominant party is on top, usually talking gross." How it feels so good: "Someone really likes missionary position enjoys it because of full-body touch and face-to-face affection," she explains.

"It helps certain aspects to be quite relevant and provides a bit of power play: hands overhead and tied reveals the breasts and giving them somewhat of a sense of ravishment. When anyone enjoys submission, immobility and ravishment are typically part of their enjoyment. The 'top' receives a delightful sensation of dominance, and the 'bottom' is there for taking — very literally."

## Queening in Bondage

"The male (or submissive partner) is on the bottom with this role. 'Queening' is also defined as 'sitting on his chest,' because this is an oral sex posture where the woman gets nice licks when the guy's hands are crossed around his head; she also needs to be careful not to place her weight on his arms while fitting in to be pleasurable.

"Another thing that doesn't ever attract the Fifty Shades of Grey reader is a good glance at a woman on top," she notes.

"'Queening' is a really effective taunt pose, where the highest individual nearly drops himself to the bottom individual but doesn't yet allow contact... 'before his wife asks!'

## Hands Behind Ankles

"Lay down to the floor or bed on your butt. Bend your knees and stretch out to your feet. Add restraints to your wrists so that they rest behind your ankles," says the certified wedding and family therapist. It extends the hip flexor muscles and flexes the glutes to a fantastic and quite arousing stretch that allows blood flow to the pelvis, "she says.

## Legs Up, Wrists to Knees

The positioning of the legs-up is really useful. As used with a spreader bar, intimacy during sex is incredibly favorable being face-to-face, without the risk of demurral. It offers the ideal goal for bastinado when used with ankles together, as seen here.

The degree of impotence generated is proportional to the height the feet of the subject is elevated to. However, one needs to be cautious not to lift the rope too far to prevent hurting the back of the neck.

There are other forms you can lock your hands in. Now they were attached to the cords about the ankles, with the last knot placed behind the knees to be beyond the control of their fingertips. It can even be tied with the arms attached to "hugging" the legs quite effectively. Chloe Says: "I just enjoy being bound in the air like this with my legs. With Bastinado, Hywel uses it a lot as the soles of my feet are vulnerable, and I am not big enough to keep touching with my hands. It's pretty easy as well (unless anyone hits the feet's soles, obviously!) and I like the fact it allows me lots of space to fight and move into various situations without being afraid to run. It always sounds a bit like a semi-suspension, except it's more manageable than others. And since my legs are bound together, it looks more damsel-in-distress than other roles do. "

## Yoke

Usually, this role is accomplished by utilizing the so-called yokes apply, as shown here. It may also be done by using ropes connected to a pole (typically a length of bamboo is used), but here one needs to be cautious if the pole is to be placed at the height of the neck-as often one has to be very wary about any rope-work or neck-limitation.

The yoke was used in the BDSM-themed film "The Secretary," most noticeably in the teaser thereto, where the mix of allowed flexibility and utter awkwardness was well proven. The subject's fingertips are open and unregulated, helping her to compose, wash dishes, cook food, and conduct certain domestic and menial tasks in all manner. She can't keep her hands close to her lips, though, and she can't feed herself quickly or with some sort of decorum, and she has to take great caution in walking about because the yokes are always too large to go through the gate.

This is also seen as a teaching tool, which is useful in calming down the slavegirl to ensure she takes good care of her duties, which exercises due consideration. The variant seen here includes heavy leg irons for more restriction; the protagonist is forced to walk at a fairly sedated speed and, therefore, can be very effective during poise, stance, and gait exercise, ensuring she walks with proper deliberation and decorum.

## Crab tie

The crab chain attaches the wrists of the slavegirl to her ankles and normally (as here) introduces binding loops at the stage of knees and elbows to hold her lower arms parallel to her lower legs. It is extremely restricting when bound properly and snugly, enabling just the opening and closure of her legs, and turning onto her back. The subject seen here was unable to fight the urge to show off by hitting a semi-standing pose, but she was highly insecure, so that would not be suggested. Chloe says: "I've just heard about this role! I don't think that's really much seen, so I certainly want to do some. I think it will be perfect for sex (as long as the tied-up person's arms weren't broken) because I appreciate how little rope it

requires – it's really inexpensive because of elegant-looking. It's one of those ties that can't resist looking pretty sexy, so I really enjoyed posing like this – particularly when it makes a lot of struggle and rolling around that I often love! "

**Bent Over The Chair**

The existence of a piece of furniture as plain as a chair brings up several new possibilities for slavery. This is only one of the hundreds of variant chair relations that can be found. For a more detailed overview of chair relations, we will ask the patience of the reader, which will be discussed in a forthcoming addition to this lexicon. Chloe Says: "Ah, I love this – one of my favorite BDSM experiences is bent over furniture – I guess it's possibly because I enjoy being spanked and canned too much, so this is one of my favorite positions for feeling powerless. I haven't been bound up like this too much, and while I'm at work, bondage and spanking don't always happen at the same moment, but I'm certainly a fan of the connection. "

**Waitress**

The posture of the waitress applies to any stance where the elbows are limited behind the back; however, the wrists are tied in front. To achieve the result, a bar was used here. The name comes from the idea that such a bound slavegirl can conveniently hold a tray of beverages in which to please customers, but can't do anything else besides.

Note that the humerus doesn't twist, and only slavegirls who can bring their elbows together behind their backs would allow the rope to be bound in this role with a spacer cinch. Chloe says: "I don't like being forced to do something useful when I'm tied up – it's very hard work and very tiring! But unfortunately, this bind allows it difficult to do all sorts of valuable tasks, while also being most obviously limited. I consider it more stressful than any other job, and I never plan to do it. Yet, at least if you were bundled up like this, you might probably make an effort to get free, which is also a relief. "

**Double V**

In front of her body, the slave-girl's arms are bound together to create two mirrored V-forms. Although requiring her to shield herself from indignity, at first sight, attaching a tight rope from the lowest point of the V serving as a crotch rope allows any protective reaction from the topic to impose a frictional price on her reputation, as well as completely restricting her freedom of movement.

The subject's legs are seen crossed here; a more drastic alternative may be to bind her legs in half or complete lotus pose, holding a binding cord to the bottom of the V's to stop inappropriate postural relaxation.

## 3.2 Erotic Spanking

**Why Spanking Is Sensual**

Some may consider a lover's spanking is a little strange or even forbidden, but obviously, a decent spanking in the bedroom has its benefits. Indeed, after the release of "Fifty Shades of Grey" a couple of years ago, increasing plenty of people want to perform this form of kinky action.

Why spank, you ask? Oh, damn, it feels fine! The buttocks are fleshy and round, as opposed to other erogenous areas. This implies for most people that a reasonable amount of pressure on the bottom is not just tolerable but also sufficient to offer pleasurable sensations. And, since the old derrière is an enticing place for many women, a nice spank may be the perfect way to light it up. Often, the act of spanking itself has not-so-subtle tones of domination and obedience, which in and of itself can be oh-so-sexy. If you're trying to introduce a little spice to your sex life or want a soft-core BDSM flavor, spanking might just be the thing for you and your partner to do. However, the best strategy and strategies are important components to render a decent spanking a sexy activity.

**Talk First, Spank Later**

Communication is necessary whether you want to offer a couple of hard slaps to your mate-or obtain any of it yourself. If the sentiment isn't reciprocal, an unwelcome spanking may be a real slap in the face. Bring up spanking gently with your partner until you pull out the whips and paddles, to try things out. You will then explore how you really feel about spanking, and maybe try it out.

Looks bad, what do you think? So, he or she doesn't want to give the partner a blow. Consent is important. And it's the perfect foreplay to decide what you intend to do to each other! (Find out how to broach the subject in Yeah! Why Acceptance Is So Sexy.)

**Play by the Rules**

Spanking can be mentally as well as emotionally traumatic. A lot of people want to experiment with the limits between discomfort, retribution, and enjoyment, so it's important to establish the guidelines in advance. Indeed by this rule, all those who enjoy BDSM abide. Then talk about the boundaries. Tell your partner if you intend to try out. And then remind them what you are not going to do, at all. Then listen to your partner for getting their point of view.

You're not, of course, trying to injure someone (much). However, an accident does happen. For this purpose, a safeword is important. This is a term or expression you wouldn't usually utter about anatomy. A traffic light's colors-red, yellow, and green-make it an outstanding safeword scheme and are commonly utilized in the BDSM culture. "Red" indicates that all operations will be suspended immediately; "gray" implies slowing down or calming off. "Green" goes without saying, means get your spank on!

**Set the Mood**

Like any erotic activity, setting the mood before you let your partner's behind you loose is important. If he or she is not sufficiently excited, then the spanking is not going to be erotic, just painful-and not in a good manner.

Going slow is best, and let the festivities progress naturally. Start with a bit of cuddling and hugging, then proceed to the foreplay. A little hint of dirty talk can really help set the mood too, especially if there's a particular naughty person.

**Get In On the Act**

If you decide to indulge your spanking dream, role-playing isn't strictly essential, but it can definitely be a nice way to contribute to the overall experience. In reality, being the spanker or the spankee can be better when you're taking the time to get into character.

Any form of role-playing domination and obedience is ideal for a spanking night. Any of the prime illustrations are owner and servant, instructor and student, or role-playing dad and little kid. You just know what kind of plot you're going, acting out. You have a lot to pick from when it comes to spanking roles. The over-the-knee posture possibly is the most rising spanking posture. Here the spankee is draped over the lap of the spanker. It is easy, intimate, and sexy.

## Assume the Position

There is, of course, more than one form of flogging a partner. There are plenty of options to pick from if the over-the-knee stance doesn't do it for you. Try leaning the spankee over a piece of furniture, standing and leaning against the wall, kneeling on their hands and knees, or lying on the bed or floor facing down.

## Get Warmed Up

Spankers: Slow-start. It's better to fire up the companion sufficiently before the serious walloping begins. Start first with sweet, gentle caresses. You will build your way up to soft swats, and eventually to a nice, full-blown spanking if your spouse responds well.

## Experiment With Technique

Not all spanking methods are made the same, so a bit of experimenting in this area can help you, so your partner discover the ones that fit better. The methods of spanking can be modified every so often by changing the form of the palm, strength, and pace of your blows. Cupping the hand when spanking, for example, would typically result in a duller, deeper thud rather than the stinging feeling that normally comes from spanking with a smooth palm. Alternating between caresses and swats, or gripping the

buttocks tightly at the end of each movement is both perfect ways to change things up a bit. Often, don't be reluctant to play with the swats as opposed to making the hand gently rebound off the buttocks, because each of both approaches creates entirely different stimuli. Listen above all about how the partner is reacting and react to it.

There should be an erotic spanking ... Okay, some are sexual. Be sure to add some sensual activity into the spanking, particularly when you assess the desire for pain that your partner has. You might scratch, tickle or rub the buttocks between spanks, for example, or stroke the anus or genitals while spanking. With a little preparation and adequate instruction, spanking alone will make someone orgasm!

Pain may be fun, but wound means you have gone past the limits. Keep spanking down to the fleshy buttocks section. It may be very difficult to spank on bony regions, such as the tail bone and hip bones, and also leave a hideous bruise. Never, ever spank a partner just over the ass, because that may contribute to damage to the spinal cord or kidney.

The spanked spouse shouldn't dread talking through the spanking sessions and be able to say their spanker when it's too severe. Additionally, the spanker will obey the rules of the spankee, and avoid spanking until the safe word is said.

The time after a session of spanking is almost as critical as the spanking it-self. This is a chance to chill, unwind, and think about what all of you loved-and didn't like. If the spanking session was particularly painful, a bit of cuddling might be in order. Even a warm bubble bath or cold washcloth on the buttocks is really relaxing, and during a spanking session may be an ideal way to bond.

Spanking can be arousing, exciting, and oh-so-sensual. When your option is a little (or a lot) of discomfort, you may want to bend over and consider spanking. Or maybe give your friend a swat or two.

## 3.3 Whipping

**Types of Whip**

We know you're anything but whipped hot! So, it's necessary for all of you wearing the pants to have every detail before you pick your dangerous tool.

We suggest a flicker whip for beginners, as it's simpler to manage than remaining, more versatile. Avoid bullwhips, until you are practicing well in advance. There will be no more than four steps to the first whip.

Usually, the whips consist of a stick, a thong, a dropping, and a popper/cracker. Bullwhips, stock whips, and snake whips have a gap between the popper and the thong that defends against damage, although other whips have no dropping. Whips are like solid tools for immediate contact or lightweight devices that have to be shaken to be successful in any way.

### 1. STOCKWHIP

They'll be an important part of your game! The method with this whip is much simpler to master than with a bullwhip, but this style of a whip is often less flexible. It can create a little effort crack, instilling terror anywhere in the bottoms, and a noisy noise can be made with a quick fish rod cast motion. This whip has a thick, stiff handle enabling fast grip and optimizing power. You're certainly going to want this frightening device!

### 2. BULLWHIP

Tops when seeing this kind of whip, it's similar to a red rag for a bull! Please just consider using a bullwhip, though, use it if you've had extreme experience before the first usage. Standing at a fetish workshop is the perfect place to practice the bullwhip. It varies from the stockwhip in that the thong and the handle from similar plait are made, or handle continuation is the thong. A flexible whip, so when we tell we don't speak bull, it's not for starters!

## 3. Snake Whip of Black Color

Would you just want your tongue to stick out at the bottom? This whip could then be the device you're searching for! While comparable to the bullwhip in nature, more robust is the handle and mounted onto the weapon. This whip is quick, short, and severe, so using it only after extreme practice. It is a slick little tool, and learning techniques will take time, and we definitely wouldn't suggest it for the first time to you.

## 4. Signal Lash/Whip

For a warning how's this? Very famous Whipping enthusiasts pick is this whip. Yet power can be fairly complicated and is not suitable for beginners as well. This implement's configuration indicates a handle is not present, but thong is loaded with shot instead. In length, it is considerably shorter, just like the black snake and bullwhip in architecture. These whips don't possess a slip between the thong and the cracker, which ensures wear & tear may be much more serious. With this strong signal, they are not going to out!

## 5. Pocket Snake Whip

This whip is like a little snake that will curl so tightly in the pocket so it can fit! So now you can have fun everywhere you go. No handle is present in

this whip; only a shot filled thong, identical in style to the signal whip. The crack created might not that much loud as its large equivalents, because this whip is very tiny in scale. But managing and monitoring this is a simple, good option for beginners. Liable to hiss the bottoms, be alert try not to slither free!

## 6. Flicker Lash/Whip

Turn on the switch between ' BDSM play' and 'play' To beginners, this Whip is the preferred device. The rigidity ensures that it is relatively easy to manage, so it is possible to learn the technique without difficulties. Extreme pain it causes, but less serious than any of the instruments listed above. This whip has no dropping, which means the thong is attached directly to the cracker/popper. This will trigger wear & tear to be greater and quicker. The hope flicker in eyes would certainly go out with this tool after a continued chastisement!

## 7. Quirt Whip

This resembles a stockwhip but has a forked tail. It's tiny in size; it's comparatively smooth and painful very much like many whips. The handle and core usually are crafted from leather. Ideal for newcomers to help them get used to whipping-related sensations. Although in comparison to counterparts it is less severe, surely this whip has extra character!

## 8. Dragon Tail Lash/Whip

Will you try to control your own inner beast? This whip isn't your solution then! That form of a whip is strong, robust, and built to provide an all-powerful snap, sure to bring out your wild side. The basic construction element simply involves a thong and a handle; furthermore, the tail (thong) in a triangle shape in sharp position tapers, produce a crack that is supremely satisfying. The whip is fairly easy to handle and is an excellent option for starters and promises that fired up all of you can.

### Whip Materials

#### 1. Nylon

The content may be synthesized, but the whip of nylon would certainly allow you to carry out all your primal impulses! These whips are very strong and simple to hold. And, with the slightest amount of treatment, they will last a lifetime. They generally deliver short, powerful, and sharp strikes and are rigid so controlling is easy.

## 2. Leather

A whip of leather is the tool for delivering a perfect chase. Durable and tough, if cared for correctly, a lifetime it can last. These whips are strong and with a solid consistency that helps them to give both a 'thuddy' and extreme pressure and a true 'sting.' It is necessary to make your target perfect before playing due to the extreme nature of leather. One thing's certain; from you it's sure to get the animal out!

## 3. Rubber

A flogger of rubber can rebound with a pleasing pinch from the skin at the feet. Well known for its seriousness, it's just for the more seasoned people. It can even cause cuts and abrasions, so be careful and follow the mentioned safety tips for spanking. You require balls to make a go of this!

## Techniques

Do you really want something to whip they'll enjoy? You should know that the spanking is associated commonly with two sensations. These are 'thuddy' and 'stingy.' A 'stingy' sensation is most commonly correlated with whips, but others may even produce a 'thud.' On the surface, a 'sting' is felt, whereas a 'thud' gives a very solid blow, almost similarly as being very hard pushed. The style of striking you select will be decided by your favorite sound.

All we have left now is for us is the whip cracking! Don't just assume any of the essential strategies to happen. Training makes you better, but what do you expect? Only three favorites of mine are here;

## Overhand

Do not throw away all your diligent work, by not having a perfect stance! This technique demands that the elbow and the forearm in position completely, pointing to where you intend to crack the whip. When the forearm points forward, the side compensates by bending the tail of the whip. And look out, we don't want you to give doubtful signals. Behind you on the ground should be the whip laid. Drag the handle off your arm to push the thong, touching the 'happy spot' you like. Be vigilant don't go to the top; steadily and slowly build up the pressure.

**Circus Crack**

And don't be a fool and seek out this beforehand without some preparation! Drag the whip up and forward, then bring it down back to find your 'sweet spot'. The 'S 'gesture involves the whip bringing up and down the arm, then

in a single move downwards. It allows greater strength and energy, thereby creating a more extreme effect discomfort. It also has an all-powerful crack. Its is an amazing performance, which will definitely make an impact in real!

**Reverse snap**

There will not be any warnings in its direction for the bottoms! Start by forming a loop with the whip over your head. Take backward the handle and hit forwards once you've learned this. For those who use a longer whip, this is such a simple technique; however, accuracy is not always and offers incredibly sharp and intense pain. We'd suggest you steer out of this form until you're some extra experienced. We don't want you to take one step ahead and two moves back after all.

With the help of 2 boxes of cardboard and a towel or pillow, you will easily perfect your target. Range the boxes apart by around two feet and put the towel/ pillow in the center. That is going to be your goal. Once each time you will reach it, without moving the frames, bring them back jointly and start over again. The cycle is continued till you are sure the target is fine. You're just ready to start now!

**Positions**

Well, it's not exactly the territory of Kama Sutra, but when it arrives in wilful beating, there is definitely no lack of positions! What you ought to know first is your 'sweet spot' is. The most popular positions are the thighs, the buttocks, and back. Many that are true punishing gluttons would gladly tolerate a beating on the vagina or breast. If you choose one of the above, though, please hit gentle and fast. Do you know where the 'sweet spot' lies? First, they will stretch the knees and contract the glutes. Flat-foot you should be, to begin with; you can shift about and play with your feet until

you have more practice. Place the attacking arm and shoulder towards the goal with shoulder feet -apart, and knees bent slightly. Now strike, throwing your whole body weight behind it.

All right, let's discuss bottoms now! When its whipping time, our favorite place is restrained. It helps to retain the edge, particularly while driving, mitigating the chance of injury. But there are still many other roles. Why not pretend to be doggy, bent over or standing?

## 3.4 Blindfolds

A blindfold is a piece of cloth that can be wrapped around the head and put over the eyes to obstruct vision. Blindfolds are often utilized in sex play as the residual senses of scent, taste, touch, and hearing may be enhanced while the sight is blocked; others often consider the aspect of discomfort inherent in not being able to see especially exciting. Blindfolds have been so popular that they are not even known to be kinky by anyone. It's sort of "kink-light" to everyone, but we agree with Lucy Collins, who points out that once you believe that it is, everything can be kinky. We're posting a few possible scenarios use blindfolds to show it – and to include scenario suggestions as asked by readers and representatives.

Take as much or as little of this as it fits your particular preferences. Mix and match these thoughts together or only let something else be the catalyst. The entire idea is to see how to integrate blindfolds into some kinky stuff you'd want to do.

Regulation over the senses of your spouse is more effective than you know. As long as everybody accepts, you should apply a blindfold on virtually everything you do to heighten their perceptions.

## Sensual Touch

It's a typical scene-a sub, bound to a pillow, a blindfold, to cover their eyes, waiting. Just ... sitting tight. Any movement triggers them to leap or to hold. The excitement and uncertainty heighten any feeling. It seems like a cliche, but it does work.

Early on in our partnership, my wife put me in such a role. It wasn't the first time I was wearing one, but it was the first time I was wearing one with her. Our exchange of power was firmly established, so I knew who would be in charge. Picture my shock, because every touch on my skin was tender, caring, and ... teasing for the next hour.

She didn't contact my dick or suck it. No nipples pinched, or even hair pulling—just soft yet strong hand-strokes. I asked for an orgasm at the end of the hour with too much focus when my body trembled. It's been more effective because it's been so soft – we're doing a hard traumatic play, and it's anything but it.

Why she did it? Other than replying to "Because you let me, baby?" Since she decided to look at me and see how I was responding to her touch. And because she could. There was nothing natural about it, but he was clearly in charge.

## Exhibitionist Play

Blindfolds seize care of your sight, which offers you more independence than you will ever imagine. Blindfolds are a choice for the exhibitionist, who is not sure whether they can withstand the truth of being exposed.

Naked on the floor or bunk, often sitting. Scarcely suited and bound to a chair. Holding horizontally, hoping to be "of use." The place in which a sub

or bottom finds itself is constrained only by what both you and your imagination relate to.

Blindfold securely in position; you require the space to get a (mutually accepted third party). Are they permitted to touch your body and pass their hands around it in ways you can't predict? Would they just watch your mate offer joy to you in whatever kinky way you want it?

The concerns, doubts, or humiliation of seeing someone seeing you have gone down. You will see nothing because you are not (consensually) in control. Now you have the right to appreciate the moment.

## Bringing in a Third...or Not

Often the actual world will be as nice-or greater than-the illusion and the imagination. Having your kinky activity by bringing in a third person can be enjoyable and exhilarating, but discovering someone you'd like to bring in on such an intimate moment isn't always convenient. And maybe you don't believe the imagination will suit reality.

Space will look and feel like more than just the two of you are there, with a blindfold and a little imagination.

Blindfold the partner, and keep them in line. Move into space, and your partner realizes you're there with ... anything to confuse them. The gag inside their mouths. A vibrator against the clit or the penis. Clamps Nipple. The kinky whispers in their ear that you can talk. Now, go back softly to the entrance, and sound like a third party has arrived.

Speak to this "guest" and start talking about your partner with them because it's obvious that they are the focus of your attention and that of your "guest." The mind is a powerful thing, and even if they know there's

no one, they might wonder, "Could it be?

**Impact Play**

Our biggest kink is impact games. It's our go-to whenever we want to play. I enjoy getting struck, and he always likes to reach me. The use of blindfolds in a scene for effect play allows it more serious.

It's cliche again, but it does work.

I often brush her gently with a doll to taunt her before taking her. So I know what is going to happen and then I can predict the effects. The little contact makes her feel damp and achy for me.

Blindfolded, she is not really sure of where I am around her, particularly for a BDSM club scene. The music is heavy so that I can't listen. I have access to 360 degrees, which ensures I maybe everywhere. And just because I softly brush her with one hand of a robot doesn't mean that's when the first hit would fall.

The lack of understanding of what is to come or when it will fall intensifies her reaction. It's still a shock, and even more intense. Her entire body responds in surprise-hard nipples and soaking cunt, but also goosebumps and sweating, and with a little fear, she might or may not bite her lip with curiosity. It is fantastic!

Blindfolds earn a poor name for being cliched or dull. And they may be. You might have attempted them a long time ago, and you really weren't aware of it. As long as this isn't a tight threshold, try it again.

It doesn't have to entail harsh orders, rigid obedience, or strong procedure to gain power over your mate. Often it's as easy as withdrawing their sight and shocking them with any touch for a moment.

## 3.5 Clips and Clamps

Nipple Clamps are uncomfortable. They are built for that. And if you are with someone who often loves the feeling, it's enjoyable during pain playing.

The level of discomfort depends greatly on the kind of clamp you have, when the clamps are placed on the body, and for how long the clamps are used on the body.

You check a grip between your index finger and thumb on the tiny piece of tissue. It is not a little bit of delicate skin, and it is really short. When you're using several clamps on it, you will know whether it's a really painful clamp or not too harsh. You should even test to see whether the clamp is simple to loosen or requires a bit more power.

Obviously, the clamping power is there, too. I don't know if that is an approved term, so the tighter the clamp sticks on, the more uncomfortable it becomes. You've got adjustable clamps too. For, e.g., in this case, you will see a little screw that can be used to loosen the clamp a little bit. That would relieve the strain on the clamp resulting in far less discomfort.

A clamp's diameter helps a lot too. A wide, flat clamp distributes the weight over a wider area, rendering the clampless uncomfortable than a comparable yet rather narrow one. And a teeth clamp hurts a lot worse than a smooth-faced grip. That makes a big difference!

## Where Can You Use Clamps?

There are other areas where you can bring the squeeze. Often men go to the vulnerable areas like the boobs, the labia, and the scrotum. But you've ever heard of placing a clamp on an ear lobe, lower lip, nose, nostril or septum,

chin, neck, chest, thighs, head, feet, and if anybody's got enough: on the foreskin. So give someone an erection instead. Nice stuff! ·

## And Where Should You Not Use Clamps?

 Knee back, armpits, buttocks, and tendons like the Achilles heel on the ankle. Sometimes, other areas including moles, zits, other irregular growths, recent tattoos (not older than 6 months), etc. If you raise the nipple a little, you may even add a little clip behind the nipple. This creates a huge difference in the degree of discomfort it induces. The piercing nipples make a difference, too. The skin between the piercing and the clamp is stretched with a piercing (at any place), which may inflict additional discomfort.

There are a few places you shouldn't be using a clamp-on.

• While applying a clamp on a man's scrotum, make sure that no vas deferens trapped in there.

• The only location in the body where muscle tissue specifically connects to the skin.

• Rough clamps cannot be used on the face (but you can always be cruel when it comes to the lips and tongue), and certainly not on the eyelids.

• How broad is the clamp base, or how fine are its edges?

• Within a clitoris, there are twice as many nerve endings relative to a full male penis, and you may want to be vigilant of this as well as making sure that the piece of skin you are using is not too small. The fewer skin that falls between the clamps, the more it has to involve. Because that clamp is about to clamp!

**Putting on a Clamp**

The procedure is simple: pull the skin up and add the clamp. You can place several clamps on it too for a pleasant feel!

Pay attention when using lubes: a clamp can fly off involuntarily when the skin or fingers are oily. Ohh!

**Removing a Clamp**

Timing is crucial. If you placed a clip on the skin, the blood at that section of the body is forced back. You'll also find that the skin is becoming whiter. If this occurs, then it hurts. When this occurs, you won't feel it anymore after a moment. But the clamp is still on. And even if you're not really noticing it, the impact will get worse.

The blood begins running back as you remove the clamp, and with that, the sensation too. Then it hurts! The longer a clip is kept on, the more uncomfortable it would be if you remove it. How long you should keep it on for each person differs. This can last 20 seconds, 2 minutes, etc.

That's why you want all clamps off before you hit orgasm. It will cause extreme pain if you are already relaxed, and you still need to loosen a clamp.

If a clamp unintentionally hurts as you release it, it will either pinch or pressure the spot where it hurts, through your fingertips. And then discharge very gradually. This means the blood will gradually and not immediately circulate back.

It also hurts a lot when you drag or touch a clamp without releasing it first. The clamp would instead in the last second bring all the clamping energy on a really tiny bit of flesh. This is extremely painful. This could be deliberate but pay particular attention to keeping anything from occurring .

accidentally. It's even harder when a lock tends to be trapped too. On the very small bit of peel! Ooooooooh!

**Creativity When Using a Clamp**

With clamps you can do lots of imaginative stuff, ranging from getting fun to mean stuff.

• For example, you might keep a vibrator against the clamps.

• You should add a thin piece of fabric or linen to the clamps too. You may do some fun with this. You will try to tear off the clamps with the ropes quite easily. Everything is likely because it's going to hurt a lot.

• You can put a number of clothespins next to each other on a string and then take them all off at once. If you see the picture, you will know why they name it "the zipper! "And if you're into that stuff, you should even use a whip to strike the body's clamps. Ooooooooh!

• You may have seen the clamps in between, with a small chain. This chain gives the clamps more weight, as well as some additional movement.

Imagine this: you are taking a few clamps that you can put, for example, on the nipples of your sub. Have a chain in between large enough to apply a little weight too and place in your sub's mouth, or it can be kept between the teeth. Good, huh? Now make your sub hurtful or tickle your sub with the chain to see how the sub tries to hold the mouth locked. And if it falls in weight and cord ... Ouch!! · It's fun (mean) to see someone crawl with clamps on. As the chain will begin to dangle, which can create some odd movements. And you don't want to walk with your knee on the chain. Yeah, will someone give me the weight of a little haggling?

## Risks

Why continue with breast injury right away? Yeah, because you can put nipple clamps on the breasts. And some people get really "excited" at the sensation.

For strong clamps, not many things will possibly go wrong. Clearly, you will damage the skin of the breasts or damage the mammary glands if you purchase clamps from some DIY shop and use them on breasts. Nonetheless, breasts can sustain a lot of pain.

Especially when you don't place the clamps directly on the nipples but placed them on the areolas instead. This way, not much will go wrong. It's always smart to keep engaging with your companion and avoid keeping them on for long at the start . 10 minutes approx.

1. Doing so much pain to others that it ceases being enjoyable for another person, and that person doesn't want to play with you again. That's a shame because anytime somebody asks you to use them, it's a lot of fun, and you want to hold the connection. So, maintain a balance in which it doesn't get too dull, but particularly, it doesn't get too stressful that someone doesn't trust you anymore.

2. The second risk is that a piece of skin will be cut off from enough blood supply for too long, causing it to die from within. It doesn't happen quickly, especially when you are communicating while doing it, but let's look at the contributing factors.

The more responsive the skin is, the more it hurts as you receive the squeeze. Which needs daily checks on it.

How strong is the movement of blood in the skin when you use the clamp?

Which skin form is it? For, e.g., the surface of the inner labia is more sensitive, so the softer surface is more susceptible to clamp pressure in this case, for, e.g., you should use the clamp on this for a shorter time than on a nipple. Obviously, if you tease it too much, you can destroy anything. And much of the time, for the sake of getting fun together, you do these sorts of stuff.

Always bear in mind the clamp's properties: how much force will it produce?

How strong is the spring?

How much extra weight is used?

People often use alligator clips from the electronics store, but they are really (really!) serious ones that can start scratching into a person's skin quite quickly – Particularly when you start pulling them.

Less intense pressure emerges from a large flat collar, covered with silicone or acrylic. An alligator clip with sharp teeth might not have a solid spring, but its teeth might be mean. Such clamps (side clamps, also called American clamps or clover clamps) are clamps that lock on tighter the harder you move it ... fun to play with on the previously described skin (not the muscle) between the thumb and index finger foundation. There's also a perfect spot to check what sort of clamp you're handling here.

The most critical advice is: At the outset, be a little more cautious. As well as that, work all the time at communicating, always testing what you are doing when you are doing it.

Enjoy the discomfort that it brings, and you can hold the grip a bit longer while you know how to understand somebody's reactions. Yet next time,

you should still be a little bit meaner and search for the biological limits more.

There's something you can do really good here that unlocks the clamp, enabling blood supply to resume and allow blood to pass across the skin (painful) and then bring the lock back in position. As I mentioned earlier, it's especially painful, but at the same time, knowing what you're doing is a good trick.

## 3.6 Collars

Normal BDSM partnership is made up of the partner dom and sub (but not restricted to such positions alone).

BDSM collar is weared by few submissive to display in partnership with their slave or submissive status.

We have marriages and wedding rings in relationships usually, and here, we have a BDSM collar in D / s relationships.

Some sub wear lockable collars to further accentuate the transition of authority to the subordinate that retains the key, whereas some do not carry the key every time.

BDSM Standard collar

While there isn't formal BDSM collar law in the culture, there is certainly a certain "norm."

Leather collars in black is wear by some subs, with metal rings attached.

Why attach a ring? Metal rings often in BDSSM collar are added to them to enable protection to be applied.

Often, however, in public, subwear something more fitting.

In this case, they carry a plain choker or chain, but there are a few degrees of the importance of BDSM collars due to similar factors.

Collaring stages

BDSM collars have some degree of significance.

This method is now commonly practiced in the community of BDSM, it is essential to other cultures and observe three collaring stages as follows.

Collaring stages:

- Consideration of Collar

- Collar Training

- Collar Slave

Consideration of collar is the First on the chart, and people generally equate it to the rings of pre-engagement. The word "collar of thought" originates in the culture of Old Leather of Guards.

It doesn't need to be a real belt. It's a necklace, a wrist band, or like anklet occasionally. A blue color leather collar will be the standard collar of attention.

By embracing the collar of attention, this collar form is given by the dom to display his concern in the sub, and the sub demonstrates that it is equally important. Through doing so, the sub is no longer eligible for a considerable time, and no respectable Dom does not seek the sub.

If this doesn't work out, the sub will eliminate the consideration collar anytime they like and terminate the BDSM connection to act like that.

The second level of collar preparation is collar training. A rough analogy is there to rings of engagement, or we might say an agreement is represented to teach and learn between a Dominant one and a sub. Dominant, at this point, is training the sub to the expectations he requires.

The partnership can still be broken, but the split is traumatic because their bond at this stage becomes deeper.

The Dominant and sub usually in length talk engages to explore the needs, desires, and lifestyles of each other to see further if they're a good combination. Perhaps they engage themselves in some of the lighter, D/s relationship vanilla aspect to find a sub's initial limits.

Usually of leather, the traditional collar is made, colored in black or red.

The final stage is the Slave collar -like a wedding ring. When dominant and submissive have progressed through "Training collar" and "Collar of consideration." Then offered this collar.

Today, the sub is the dominant's, official slave. BDSM groups following these phases perceive this partnership stage, as irreversible, with little possibility of stopping it.

The dom can, in a special situation, terminate the relationship.

**Collars Info**

Leather, plastic, stainless steel, and PVC are the most popular materials though leather is a "king" definitely.

Its also growing that the collars are used as fashion accessories, and in this case, cotton, neoprene, nylon, are typical fabrics.

The BDSM collars may be adorned with pins, studs, or screws, which also contain buckles, padlocks, belts which chains, and other accessories.

Different collars Types as follows:

- Wolf collar

- Halter collar

- Posture collar

- Day collar

- Turian collar

**Wolf collar**

Wolf collar is with hoops on it, studs, and spikes. It is typically used to defend dogs from wolves – that's where it earned the label. The features of a dog collar are called glamorous in the context of BDSM.

Any versions of the Wolf collar include plastic, spikes, and nails and only for safety purposes, while natural spikes, nails, and studs can be harmful.

**Halter collar**

It is also a drop collar, that falls low on the front. Like Turian collar it is as free is the neck to move, and wearing for long periods can be more secure.

They are typically designed in such a manner that conveniently you can hold on the drop lowest part of any other item of jewelry.

**Posture collar**

It is a form of corset system designed for the neck, rather than the chest. It doesn't pinch the back since the chest is squeezed by the standard corset. The pose collar, as its name implies, helps preserve the stance by holding the head high and stretching the neck.

## 3.7 Male Chastity belt

Trying orgasm and chastity, denying all, is common for people. While getting first denial time locked in some system may seem really pleasant, the fact is that you still aren't ready. Managing a system of chastity is, in itself, a great change. If your need to climax still distracts you, it will not make easier things. Try, first, to abstain for some days. Even if you've never denied it before, without any problems of self-discipline, you should for one week go. My first duration of denial was about 2 weeks, and this was perfect. Once you have achieved this and used to this abstinence-accompanied feelings, you'll be ready for an actual device trial.

**A device of the proper size?**

Many people are buying devices that don't fit properly that will cause problems, big ones, or a small one. It isn't easy to buy the proper size. You may not actually know what size is required until you try one. That's why purchasing a computer that's adjustable for the first time is always easiest. The device's cage portion isn't that important as the back ring, so multiple rings devices such as the Bon4 and the CB-6000 are superb. If very tight the cage is or very big, it does not bring any pain to you. However, the wrong size back ring, will chafe a number, break off or, even worse, prevent blood supply and may cause injuries. A device having a lot of rings you can afford then doing so I suggest.

## A device of the proper style?

I'll assume you will buy a "ball-trap" device of some standard because it's your first device. The most common option, the cheapest and realistic options these are. You could, of course, for a complete locking belt go

straight, but at least at first most people will not want lengths like these. So what tool is that for you? I'll assume you've measured it already yourself (while flaccid) and got an idea that the size device you're looking for. But style is also important many designs are there, with each having benefits and disadvantages.

The devices the Bon4 and the CB-6000 are comfortable, but they are pretty close together. That means you cant wear them for an indefinite time because you have to clean the device and yourself. They're going to be good for a couple of days (providing you're thoroughly cleaning yourself), but you can't put them on forever. You'll need a metal crafted device to have a design more open.

Steel appliances (often plated with chrome) are cheap relatively but will get rust with time. Devices of stainless steel are a bit more expensive, and the titanium devices are more expensive.

There are a lot of vendors who can give you a fully personalized design to suit your choice metal perfectly, but they are pricey. To start with, when you remove it for cleaning every day is not the way completely(e.g., like an online keyholder), it is probably best to have a sealed system with lots of different sized choices, at least before the required size is known by you (when to request a custom model if you choose).

Please note that no this type of device is going to be 100 percent protected, and making it PA piercing secure, it will not stop you from reaching orgasm. A complete belt system even can't stop orgasm if you're keeping against it a Hitachi Magic Wand. This suggests still some control is needed in yourself. The good thing is that it will get easier with time, so hang on to it, and you're going to be fine.

**Skin preparation**

Many buy and just place chastity tools on, trusting devices to perfectly work without any additional work. That's like having an immense anal dildo without lube, assuming nothing different. Preparation can really make a big difference. Trim your hair for the first time, so it is thin but not absolutely straight around your waist. Yeah, becoming completely smooth while wearing a computer looks sexy. That is definitely the way we want it to be. Though, if used for the first time an irritation will be the result as you're not going to be familiar to rubbing your skin against the ring. It will be prevented by cropped hair from getting the device tangled and accidentally being pulled. It also will have a tiny amount of back ring security to help avoid chafing.

Another thing required is to add a lube before you put it on. I believe water-related lube is the simplest approach and the best mess-free one. As for liquid Organics, anything dense would fit good. Applying to skin some lube will allow to moves freely the device, as you like. You don't want the tool to fall off because if it can't function, then there's going to be a surface layer that can't breathe. To apply and reapply lube as needed is often a smart idea, but necessary for silicone tools such as Bon4, as they're more grasped than their metal or polycarbonate equivalents.

**For the first time Don't keep it on for very long.**

Purchasing a gadget may seem really sweet, and then literally give the key to wife or partner. Unfortunately, dreams are all visions. In fact, you're going to need a little time before you're ready for this. Springing right into chastity 24/7 can create trouble for you.

First, do it for a limited amount of time (e.g., an hour). Take off the mask for 1 to 2 hours, and provide the skin a rest for some time (you can still wear it back afterward). Keep it on throughout the first time, periodically assess your feeling. For the first time, at home, you should so regularly check yourself to have an idea if that fits well. Remember that you'll be quite turned on when you wear it for the first time and wider than normal (it took a lot of days for me to master it).

You can come down to normal, which can take some time. That is the scale by which you must be calculating. When all is fine, check that the correct size of the ring is there or not. If a lot of rings are there then if necessary, you can choose the correct one. Once you've got the correct one of your size, now you can start increasing the wearing time. If you've done a few hours, and it's all right, why not attempt a full day?

Make sure to have some lube (since you'll probably need it a couple of times) also a backup key if it's too uncomfortable, and you have to extract it rapidly (do not attempt, the spare key, and only in emergency use it). Take it off when going to sleep once you have done a whole day and allow your skin another break and in the morning wear it again.

## Don't go to sleep while wearing it.

You should consider wearing it overnight after having at least two days without a complaint. If you aren't used to it so, it would be very difficult to sleep with it on. I'm not trying to deceive you; it's the toughest thing to acclimate to sleep. Your body can have erections at night, so while you're sleeping, you won't be able and reapply lube, all of which don't make it simple.

Give an hour or some more time off to yourself before bed when you are able and wear it back before turning out the lamp. Apply enough of lube and seek to relax beforehand. Normally, I don't suggest masturbation in chastity blogs, but one time is this (if you're allowed) where granting an orgasm to you can benefit you because your body won't have that many erections like you haven't when ejaculated for a while. If you even have an orgasm in advance, first night of your might not be entirely comfortable, but on a Friday night do it or on holiday, or at that time when laying in and a partially-sleepless night will not hurt you.

If you awaken by an erection at night time, don't worry, that's natural. Laying down there and assuming it will quickly go away might seem the best solution, usually, it never succeeds. The best thing is to head out for a stroll outside. If you're able to get to the restroom, that'll help too. A bladder fulled completely may put pressure on the penis, which is the reason of erections at night time. Going to the restroom will relieve this, and by a walk also can make you get flaccid again quickly. It will take longer to lie still, and can be uncomfortable.

If noticed by you that you can't go to sleep again, allow yourself a rest, disable the tool, and try the next night again. But don't indulge in it for some more days. You are going to need to power on after that and go through it all night. Don't stress; until you're familiar with it, it is a lot better. You can quickly sleep through the night!

## The spare key is important

The sight of a key hanging around your Mistress' ankle might be the reason for your entry in chastity, have an extra key at the door, or should have a fast way of breaking this (emergency).

This can be done in a lot of ways and also kept secure. Those single-use, tamper-proof plastic locks can be used. They're not pricey, so your babe will remember the serial no. and see for how much time you're going to carry it on. They are fantastic but perhaps a little wasteful before you wear the tool for some days at least.

An extra key inside a safe little box may be a smart plan. Now, you need only a fast way out of your keyholder to get the combination. If they're at a corporate conference, they might not get absolutely pleased to disrupt that. Like I have done things in past times and are in a locked box, getting an extra key. For additional peace of mind, you may ask the keyholder to write their name on the lock. If you hold that with you, you are never going to be in some harm position.

But, a device of polycarbonate you have such as strong CB-6000, the cage rods can be snapped by you into the previous ring in an utter emergency. However, this may become costly and very risky. Holding an extra key is the only path ahead before you are fully assured that you will be willing to rock your watch forever.

## Take your moment.

It might be taken incredibly well by you into the unit. I think It was so excited to be trapped in the chastity and that result in sleeping in it, and then worked past the few sleepless nights. This was definitely not the right decision in retrospect, but I was interested as I am sure everyone else too!

However, if it takes some extra time, don't stress. Don't just give up. Keep going ahead and sleep all night with a little energy, and be able to put on the device forever ( cleaning exception) after one or two weeks.

## Just love it!

A most significant argument regarding penis chastity in this beginner's guide, and overall regarding male chastity games. Chastity is having fun! Many people instantly love it, but the ones who don't still consider it pleasurable with the passage of time. When you need some inspiration, consider how satisfied the keyholder is with you. Talk of how good the next orgasm would be, how powerful it would be for too long to ejaculate. Talk of how relaxing is having a keyholder partner willing to spend some time and energy to keep your keys. I'm confident that in time you'll learn to enjoy all chastity moments, like me.

I talk of orgasms before doing it and was mocked. Now I love the sensation of extreme pleasure very much; when I am brought to climax, I still do not like it! I felt great after 2-3 weeks in an apparatus. During orgasm and much of the time, I don't want to do that. I'd rather not trade a couple of seconds of gratification for the continuing emotions that only sustained chastity will offer.

Key with some other person. You may assume anything wouldn't require mentioning, but I'm learning every time from people that are worried or afraid about giving up the degree of power. Let remember this: The true fun starts here!

Now all starts as a fantasy. The thought of living in chastity without monthly pleasure on end is a big turn on, that you are masturbating every night thinking of it. Yet you can never know how wonderful its feeling is to be in committed chastity before you finally turn over the connection to someone literally. I'm positive you offer yourself excuses why they couldn't do it. You don't want people seeing your gadget through your shoes,

heading to the gymnasium or something. These are not reasons, these are explanations, and they are poor ones. Every day I put on my work dress with chastity below. I practice in a public gymnasium wearing it. Hiding below the towel is easy enough, and no one can watch this chastity through my dress as I am wearing tight undergarments.

Only bite the trigger, wear a full-time computer, and turn over your card. Wearing chastity is like a tremendous pleasure, but that is compounded by being personally regulated by someone several times over. You do not want to miss this!

## 3.8 Hogtied Bondage

Hogties are useful bondage accessories and make it much more fun for making ankle and wrist cuffs -if you are versatile enough.

A hogtie is leather or another kind of bondage binding substance rendered in an X shape or cross. It can also be constructed entirely out of wire or rope. There is a trigger clip or other bondage type at each four pieces end, which you may bind to the D-rings or O-rings on a willing bondage fan's ankle and wrist cuffs. In the traditional hogtied situation, it may be done either when the bound individual is faced up, pulling them in a very awkward 'dead beetle' pose, or while they are looking down with hands behind and legs extended and lifted.

## 3.9 Rope Bondage

It is an elaborate kinky practice that ends in not only reassuringly inescapable slavery but also amazing suspension forms and rope harnesses.

A Japanese rope (shibari) bondage type with, especially, creative knots. It may be challenging for a novice to achieve such complex ropework, but you're surely going to be a rope master/mistress very quickly by moving up from easy loops and learning simplified rope restraints. This type of rope may use to turn a dressed or nude person into a stunning piece of art of kinky. This rope is distinct from common rope since it is not meant to bite through the flesh. You can feel deep welts, rope burns, or worsen by using an ordinary one. There are different types at low rates available, such as silk rope and hemp rope, should you want to play with rope.

When learning and loving rope bondage, it is best to have safety scissors in pairs near at hand, and there is always an easy way to release the one tied. You do not know when the critical need can be. Remember, never increasing this rope around someone's neck to attach them, and please use only the approved knots and links in different bondage guides.

As described, these are available in different material styles and various lengths, and depends on what use you'd like. Some fans love this rope harnesses as they sit, stand, or lay down. Others love the bondage suspension part, where bondage devices or rope with the firmly best furniture and features are used, plus kinky devices such as spreader bars and anal hooks.

## 3.10 Tape Bondage

Do not ready for rope? or wire isn't your method, why don't you pursue bondage tape? No matter the size, a bondage tape role is simple to use and incredibly cheap. This smartly crafted tape is meant to adhere to itself, not to body skin, so it can be used securely except in the most vulnerable places.

It's available in a variety of funky and bright colors, also as traditional 'kinky' black.

This restricting tape can bind your companion across their ankles, wrist, and other parts, or you can opt to build a mouth gag, a safe blindfold or a very kinky and provocative outfit to wear. This tape is such a handy bondage tool that adds to the kinky box; I want everybody to must include one roll in play bag for BDSM.

## 3.11 Bars Spreader

These are constructed of stiff materials such as wire and include an inflexible bar completely intended to hold ankles or wrist tightly apart during sexual play sessions. Typically these slender yet rigid bars have O or D-rings at each hand or some kind of fastening region that can be tightly secured to your rope, bondage cuffs, or any form of restriction.

Typically this is placed between the feet, thighs, or knees of the bondage fan to hold the legs separated during the exchange of power sessions, increasing the insecurity experienced by the bound one and enabling the in charge one to assert their superiority in total independence and in highly thrilling ways. These may often be used to hold their wrists/arms separated, consenting bound human front or behind. They're great devices to hold their Dominant play partner's submissive set, open, at the mercy (consensual).

## 3.12 Restraints Under Mattress

Many people have one double bed, and a perfect way to embracing bondage is by purchasing the chains under-mattress sets that have links conveniently positioned under a mattress small, king or queen-sized. Ankle and wrist cuffs bind to tethers, restraints are then conveniently embraced before, after, or after the normal lovemaking practices or role-play selected.

Sleep restraining devices are often suitable for those lacking a headboard and used in combination with conventional cuffs, like rubber or lined. If a headboard with solid bars is present, then if these are your preferred type, I would encourage you to use soft neoprene or leather cuffs. As stated earlier in this post, metal cuffs can be very uncomfortable and may even trigger harm.

In the warmth & security of your own home, an underbed bondage re-straints package is a simple way to experience the bondage feeling of cuffs.

## 3.13 Humbler

They are another form of CBT system (cock and ball torture) that, owing to a devilishly clever nature, keeps the wearer shaped partly. They are made up of two flat, polished wood bits, specifically designed to be around the testicles and penis. One section is positioned on the testicles either side while the sub on every fours posture is. Instead, the screws are threaded on the wood pieces each side and held securely in place.

The person wearing it cannot retake a standing posture, thereby holding in a 'humble' physical pose and help to sustain a submissive mentality for the remainder of the play session.

## 3.14 Double Ended Dildos

At the same moment, these double-ended dildos join two partners. Those toys also vibrate, giving extra indulgence.

This may be used by two people (or men!), where one integrates within them the tiny sculpted end and penetrates with the base via their mate. Women will use this on male friends that choose to get penetrated as well. Standard sex positions and gestures are meant to fit well, but you can need more lube! Bend the ends, so they reach you in two positions at once for so-lo action.

## 3.15 Vibrating Panties

A very different type of hands-free vibrator, these pulsing panties make it as pleasurable to place on your underwear as it falls off.

Vibrating panties typically have to be within a certain span of turning them on from the remote or mobile. And for various conditions, there are a few common variants. Few high-tech panties deliver only a pocket for a rotating vibrator with bullets. You will move the vibrator directly to turn it on and off. Others have built-in vibrators that have a cord linking the remote to the panties. Wireless slippers are remotely controlled. Your partner will click on as a surprise during the day based on how far the remote may be from the slippers.

## 3.16 Rabbit Vibrators

What kind of rabbit should you ask? The bunny is better known to be displayed on Sex and Area, entering the vagina while fluttering on one's clitoris. This allows for the arousing of all areas at once. They typically contain or will propel, a range of speeds and settings.

Set the movements to your best moves and speed, then work your way up. Pulse the dildo end within, before you're at your most pleasurable, full pace. That can be hands-free if it thrusts.

## 3.17 Thrusting Dildos

By retracting and rotating back and forth, some of the newest and most creative sex toys to enter the market penetrate, thrusting dildos or "pulsators." They mimic penetrative sex, irrespective of whether you add them vaginally or anally.

Such evil guys take control of you, without raising a hair. A partner with thrusting dildos is typically not required, particularly if they come with a vibrator that stimulates your clitoris, rabbit-style.

## 3.18 Finger Vibrators

Generally, rubbery (or ridged) pads that you place on your fingers, these temptations transform your hands into vibrators, each finger being a dildo. They're normally made of an elastic ring with a pleasure-providing surface. The larger the projectile, the more powerful the emotions that it can offer.

Mount these shivering gadgets around your fingertips. They would also require lubricant — many finger vibrators are textured, so when used raw on a clitoris or other sensitive areas may sound rough. Trace the vibrators along with breasts, buttocks, inner thighs, and back to taunt the friend before moving it to more vulnerable places. Feel free to change where your finger perches — the lower down it lies, the further leverage you would have.

## 3.19 Dildo play

What do you say, are dildos just for masturbation? Yes ... You are incorrect, though. The dildos are often used during group play with the friend. Using a dildo while playing girlfriend will enhance your sex life together. If you've just used dildo for masturbation, then that is not your responsibility. Most people in India use only a dildo for masturbation. But let me make it explicit. A couple may use a dildo for personal gratification too.

I have been getting several questions regarding the dildo during partner play from the last few days. And if you do have some doubt regarding the dildo, then you can clear it up. It's really convenient if you choose to use your dream dildo for your partner. The only stuff you can do to accurately pick the right pair dildo with a dildo.

Now, you have a lot of doubts on your mind regarding the dildo couple or how the couple is using a dildo, which sort of dildo is better for the couple, etc. I realize you want to learn how to use a dildo in partner action too.

If you're a dildo lover and you just want a nice dildo in your personal life, then you can seek the dildo while playing partner. During partner sex, using a dildo is as easy as using it on its own during masturbation.

I say you can use the pair of dildo the same way you use a dildo in your masturbation period.

Choosing the dildo is the most significant aspect regarding the couple use dildo or pair dildo.

As you know, there are so many different kinds of dildo sex toys available in India and across the globe.

Yeah, determining which pair dildo is better for you if you haven't had a lot of practice with dildo sex toys or some other sex toys is a little complicated for you.

So here we're going to add some suggestions on dildo styles that will help you get more educated and help you pick the right dildo pair.

If you are a new person or you don't have a ton of knowledge regarding the couple dildo or dildo styles, then you can pick the tiny, slimmer dildo with a buddy for your first dildo use. There's even an alternative for novice users to choose the easy and compact dildo.

If you and your partner are still involved in using the dildo, then it is necessary to get the right model if you decide to engage yourself in anal dildo pair intercourse than you can pick the anal dildo.

Anal dildos are typically slender while dildo used to enter the vagina is accessible with loads of girths.

Now a day, some of the dildos are produced in such a way that they have a practical sensation. Generally, this form of a dildo is produced from the material that looks quite close to the truth. It is born of balls of nerves, scrotum, and testicles.

Both the couple can use that kind of dildo sex toy comfortably. Whether you are in anal play or practicing pussy doesn't matter when you would like to show the practical dildo, so don't hesitate to use the condom dildo.

Much of the practical dildo with the suction cup is usable, and it is simpler to use. This form of a dildo is often used for the couple who want to get interested in the pegging with a clip-on belt.

Any special form of dildo-sex toys included in this list. Specially built for the experienced consumer, this dildo sex toy.

If you have too many dildo sex toys encounters so consider this dildo. This form of a dildo is not used on the partner on both. This is designed particularly for women's and lesbian's simultaneous vagina and penetration.

As you learn, you can invest some time on foreplay or oral sex before you get interested in penetration.

If you're a dildo enthusiast, so you know how to use a dildo to improve anticipation and satisfaction in a particular way.

Yet if you are a pair of newcomers, then you can know about the usage of the dildo. It lets you having sex with your dildo.

If you like the external and internal stimulus during oral play, then dildo is the best choice for you. Also, don't hesitate to use dildo sex dolls with a personal lubricant or a lube. Attach the dildo gradually and gently after adding the lube and push it in and out or up and down according to your preference as well as your friend.

Communicate with your spouse while engaged in an oral activity, what feels good. Glass dildo and Metal dildo are the best oral play choice. This mixture of the dildo sex toys on your wife's clitoris, and your tongue and lips also bring her special satisfaction that she never felt before and is really explosive.

If you use a dildo instead of direct contact with a penis during sexual intercourse, then it allows the sexual behavior more enjoyable.

Using and put your own dildo into the anus, then push it up then down. You should always use the hand or arm to activate externally at the same time.

When you have a cock so you can quickly remove it at any moment with the dildo, it helps you to play dominant and submissive with simplicity and protection.

A dildo may also be used for the anal activity. Just make sure you and your friend are up for it while using the dildo for anal sex.

The most significant aspects of anal play are that you can only use the anal lubricant. You should use your partner's anal dildo, or use your partner's anal dildo on you. It doesn't matter which person you are in a group.

If you don't want to mount the dildo when engaged in the anal play, so don't do it. Anal opening has an region abundant with nerves and use the dildo for stimulation and caressing. It's even bringing you the sensation of satisfaction.

You should always continue your anal play with a tiny dildo, and then step up to the bigger dildo once you get relaxed if you want the dildo products to be mounted than you want the flared based dildo.

## 3.20 What is rough sex?

Fast and hard to penetrate. We rock you to the heart with those powerful thrusts. Warm, filthy talk, punctuated with alluring, burning hand blasts. Such gestures, including extreme pain and aggressive actions against each

other by both parties, are the hallmarks of rough sex.

Although raw sex and BDSM can include both spanking and bondage elements, they are different sexual practices. The BDSM anticipation is focused on the balance of control, in which one spouse becomes superior and the other submissive. Hard intercourse is enlivened by both spouses' unbridled impulses. No one has an assertive position, either top or bottom. But it is essential for all BDSM and rough sex faith and agreement.

## What is it that people want rough sex?

Rough sex is one of the sexual fantasies, which is most common. 62 percent of women and 75 percent of men consider rough sex very attractive, according to a recent poll commissioned by an OkCupid dating app. Read on when you're ready to find out which rough sex gestures to help you combine physical power and uncontrolled desire in the most orgasmic way.

## Make Rough Sex Memorable

Crack the Barrier The act of tearing off your partner's clothes reveals lust so crazy and so intense a passion that they are unable to regulate. Because there is a fair risk that the cycle could affect the clothes, we advise you to carry one you won't regret. Inexpensive lingerie is suitable for a casual appearance without losing high-end underpinnings.

Hand restraint is one of the win-win strategies for bringing some sexy intensity to your game on how to be rough during intercourse. Consider missionary style with the partner on top keeping the hands of the bottom partner tightly over their head to provide a soft start to the rough action. The usage of soft constraints is a secure and thrilling improvement to this situation.

Incite love for your girlfriend with these gentle, flexible handcuffs. Ideal for casual physical play, they are quick to place and remove.

Rough Contact Spanking is a genuine sex maneuver. Use hands or a paddle to rub the butt improves blood supply to the region next to the penis, which in effect results in greater arousal and anticipation rates. You are beginning a reciprocal mutual conversation by playing rough with your partner's butt, so be willing to be on the receiving end should your wife want to turn the tables around and spank you again.

Hand spanking is sweet. However, it brings the play to the next stage with a paddle. Thick leather stings sweetly, heating the ass, thus producing thrilling whip-like noises when you slap.

Hard thrusting for both partners may be highly pleasurable, which is why people want to have rough sex. Close penetration for a woman offers a wonderful G-spot boost, as well as vigorous clit rubbing. If a guy penetrates, he can immerse his entire shaft for full gratification, or he can have his P-spot massaged easily if he is penetrated. Adding strong vibrations of a cock ring, in either case, would enhance orgasmic output to produce a 10 out of 10 per time.

Place on the Hero Cock Ring and adjust the speed of each hard thrust without pausing your tough session by using the remote control.

In the sense of raw sex, butt-playing unlocks the back door to a new world of pleasure. Anal adventure is one of the most fun ways to become more accessible about your desires and show your dirty, adventurous side while jazzed up with spitting and butt slapping. That, at least, is all it takes for actual material!

To easily and comfortably ready the booty for large anal, practice the sphincter for effective penetration using gradually-sized conical butt plugs.

A large, broad, and dense shaft offers intense physical gratification, as well as an enormous psychological sense of fulfillment, generating strain on both clitoris and prostate-connected nerve endings. While the typical penis has a girth of 4.59 inches, like every queen size or king knows, through the use of large toys, you will appreciate the "full-stuffed" look.

The Big Boy's huge girth, incredible length, and strong vibrations are a sure bet for experiencing the intensely rewarding feeling of being full to over-flowing-while constantly expanding yourself to take in still more.

When coupled with strong sensations, the Dopamine Euphoria Rough sex "shocks" the nervous system, triggering a rush in dopamine and endorphins. As the nerve-fired excitement builds up, every cell of your falling alive, before you eventually find yourself convulsed in mind-numbing, numerous orgasms that leave you in a state of utter ecstasy and complete fulfillment.

# ENLARGE IT!

## The Bulletproof Program to Enlarge Your Best Friend in 71 Hours

**Lil Rey**

# Table of Contents

# Introduction to the book

According to research (and perhaps to most women), men often harbor lots of secrets especially when it comes to sex. While they readily admit to these things, they are also quick to point out that most of these supposed secrets that people assume are quite frustrating. One of these "myths" that are going the rounds is that men think about sex 24/7. In defense of the men out there, they often argue that, while their minds do often stray to sex, it doesn't mean that that's all they ever think about. Women, while they're generally less likely to admit, also have numerous thoughts about sex throughout the day. It may be not quite that often but they still do (and while they're at it, why not think about the ways to help their guys up the ante in the bedroom).

Another thought that men find annoying is that sex for them, according to assumption, is just a way to get off. Men can easily get off. It's called *masturbation*. Most men are emotional too. Sex can be romantic and not just a physical activity with the goal of satisfying a need. This is true, by all means, but sex can also be a way to connect with other people. Not all men are barbarians or animals with nothing better to do than to just get off.

Many confess to imagining other people, celebrities mainly, while doing the deed. This is one secret that many men actually have.

The thing is, women are also guilty sometimes. This kind of thought is considered cheating by some. But as long as one does not put thoughts into actions, then there is no actual cheating or the cheating is minimal at the least.

Many guys (women, as well) also hide the truth from their current lovers about the number of sex partners they have had. In American Pie, there's this thing they call "The Rule of Three. This rule states that; the actual number of girls a guy has slept with will be whatever number he tells you divided by 3. Conversely, the number of guys a girl has slept with will be whatever she tells you time 3. But those rules aren't true all the time. People have different reasons why they don't admit their real number. Guys sometimes lessen their number to avoid being labeled a sex fiend or sometimes to shun a fight with their jealous partners. Women do so most likely to avoid being called easy. Sex is a natural thing. The number of people any person has slept with does not dictate who he or she is as a person. Some are just more open about their sexuality than others.

# Part 1: The Porn Stars Method to Explosively Enlarge Your Best Friend in Only 72 Hours

## Chapter 1: Introduction to Penis Enlargement

BIG is better, say many. But just as many firmly state the opposite: size doesn't matter. And then there are some who are neither here nor there, believing "it's not what you've got, but how use it that matters"

When it comes to penis size, just about everybody has got an opinion. And that's all right. Different people have different preferences.

A new study shows that women who prefer vaginal intercourse over other types of sex like it better with men with longer penises. The same feeling is echoed by women who have frequent vaginal orgasms. These women reveal they climax more easily when having sex with a man with a longer penis.

The new studies do settle the debate once and for all.

They also prove that the male anxiety about penis size is not without a good reason—bigger penis does equate to better satisfaction for many women.

This was women's perspective. What do men in general feel about penis size? (Of course, we have to ask them too — after all it is a man thing.)

Their answer is actually hardly surprising, for men being men always like it bigger.

Forty-five percent of men, a study reveals, are unhappy with the size of their penis. (Now we know what men ask for when we say to them, "Make a wish.")

So, it's all settled and proven: many women like bigger penises and many men want the same.

Now only two important questions loom large:

1. How small is small penis?

2. How do I increase my penis size?

The answers are here. Let's dig in...

## How small is small penis?

When the penis is in the flaccid state, its average length, as found by several studies, is between 3.5 and 3.9 in. On the other hand, the average length of an erect penis is between 5.5 and 6.3 in, while the average girth is between 4.7 and 5.1 in.

A penis size that is smaller than the average penis length is considered small. With that said, many men with an average or slightly-better-than-average penis believe their penis is small when it isn't.

Are there specific exercises to increase penis size?

YES. Whether your penis is small or you think your penis is small, there are exercises to increase the penis size.

Numerous exercises, when done regularly and done as directed, have shown to result in an increase in the penis size substantially. However, to enjoy the benefit, the exercises must be done 5 days a week for no less than 6 months.

The changes become visible as early as 2 or 3 weeks after starting. The real gains in the size of the penis, however, are noticed after only 6 months.

You must exercise for 1 hour 5 days a week. Two days of rest is needed. (You can take a day off on two consecutive days or on two separate days.) The rest period is crucial as it is then that the cells heal and regenerate.

## How does penis size increases with exercise?

Actually it's all science. And to understand how exercises increase the penis size, we must first understand the science behind penis erection.

The penis contains **corpora cavernosa,** spongy vascular chambers that run through the length of the penis, which when filled with blood leads to erection.

The penis enlargement exercises aim to expand the size of these chambers because an expansion will allow them to absorb more blood, which in turn will affect an increase in the penis size. By deliberately stretching tissues that cause erection, the exercises create a tensile strength, which, in turn, gradually causes an increase in the growth of these tissues.

## Statuary Warning

While each of the exercises given is safe, you are recommended to consult your urologist before doing them, especially if you have or have had any of the following health conditions:

Diabetes

Liver Cirrhosis

Respiratory disease

Any other disease which affects the flow of blood and oxygen into the penis

Don't take these symptoms lightly:

Bubbles on the penis (happens because during exercise pressure is put on the penis for a considerable length of time)

Some soreness (may happen because of repeated pulling of the organ)

Swelling on the penis

Stop exercises immediately if one or more of the aforementioned symptoms are experienced and immediately consult an urologist. Do not resume exercises until the symptoms have disappeared completely.

## Four Things You Must Do Before Performing Penis Enlargement Exercises

1. Shave off the pubic hair. We don't want you to accidentally pull it during the exercise, because it will painful.

2. Eat healthy and drink lots of water, just like you would do if you were working on your biceps.

3. Apply a moisturizer on your penis before starting. We don't recommend soap or shampoo. They can irritate the penis skin and cause redness.

4. Measure the penis. You must measure the length and circumference of penis during an erection as well as the length of penis when it's flaccid.

# Chapter 2: Hormones necessary for Penis Enlargement

Human growth hormone (HGH) is produced in the pituitary gland. As you age, the pituitary gland gradually starts to generate less of the HGH, resulting in a reduction in muscle mass and bone compactness, and escalates in fat mass. However, growth hormone can be naturally increased through weight training, aerobic exercise, appropriate nutrition and rest. Weight training assists to increase the pituitary gland to liberate the growth hormone to stimulate muscle growth and hypertrophy, as well as promotes the body to use fat as energy. When muscles contract and relax during numerous sets of weight training, the body generates hefty levels of HGH to repair and restore the tissues that have been placed under strain. HGH also increases during aerobic exercise and performing at least 30 minutes of aerobic exercise five days a week at moderate to high intensity will activate the release of HGH. Though an amplified intensity stage will promote the release of the hormone, however overtraining will do the opposite and cause it not to release. For muscle growth to happen, amino acids must be accessible in the body. Amino acids located in protein assist to restore and form muscle tissue. Guzzling a well-balanced diet involving of at least 30 percent of your overall daily calories in protein is sufficient to effectively stimulate muscle growth. Protein can originate from either plant or animal sources. However, when selecting animal sources, it is best to eat lean meats such as, lean chicken breast, beef, eggs, or low-fat dairy products. Also insufficiency of sleep or overtraining will have the opposite effect on the human growth hormone. When the body does not obtain adequate sleep or is over trained, the adrenal gland discharges the stress hormone cortisol, which triggers your body to stock more fat. For your body to generate the growth hormone, sufficient sleep is essential to promote muscle growth as a result of weight training, and the target hours of sleep should be between 7-9 hours. Exercise is one of the most efficient ways to counteract many lifestyle-related diseases. Remarkably, it can also enhance your testosterone levels. New studies in obese men propose that getting involved in more physical activity was even more useful than a weight loss diet for escalating testosterone levels. Weight lifting is the greatest form of exercise to enhance testosterone and high intensity interval training (HIIT) can also be very beneficial, although all forms of exercise should work to some degree. The human body is created in such a way that it increases stem cell quantities when we participate in more physical activity.

# Chapter 3: Natural techniques to enlarge your penis in 72 hours

There are several ways by which you can increase the length and girth of your penis naturally, it all depends on how well you penis can handle such enlargement methods without you having any side effects through mishandling of such natural methods. Learn which methods of natural penis enlargement you are most comfortable with.

Natural penis enlargement involves the use of natural formulations such as herbs, exercises, and devices. With the use of enlargement exercises, pumps, traction devices and extenders you can increase the size of your cock.

## Mechanical Penis Enlargement-Pumps, Extenders, Weights

Mechanical penis enlargement pumps, extenders and weights are some forms of physical devices which can be used in such a way that a permanent enlargement is achieved without any form of deformation or negative side effects as long as you use them correctly. Enlargement pumps, extenders and weights will improve your erection hardness, help prevent premature ejaculation, increase the length and girth of your penis, and can help straighten a curved penis.

Penis enlargement pumps, extenders and weights are generally classified as penis traction devices. They are generally less invasive compared to other forms of penis enlargement. You can achieve an elongation of your penis by up to 25% or even more depending on the effectiveness of the traction devices. Pumps, extenders and weights are also one of the best options in the increase of penis shaft for a small penis.

The **penis enlargement pump** is a cylinder which can fit perfectly well on the length of your penis, and with the help of a manual or motorized pump, a suction effect will be created on your penis. A hand pump is more reliable because you have more control over the suction. A partial vacuum is created on your penis with these pumps, and when such vacuum is created, blood will rush through the nerves, and with continuous increase in blood pressure, you penis becomes enlarged in length and girth.

**Penis extenders** are also referred to as penis stretchers. These stretches will exert continuous traction on your penis. Your penis becomes can grow in length and girth. Penis extenders will extend or stretch your penis according to the period of time the device is worn (the more you wear it, the longer and wider your penis can grow). The advantage of a penis extender is that is can be worn during day under your clothes. "Hey buddy is that a pencil in your pocket or are you just happy to see me?" Just don't get caught! A penis extender contains plastic rings and metallic rods, the rods provide the traction and with an extender you can achieve an extra 2.3cm on the length of your penis but you will have to wear it for 3-4 hours every day for up to 5 months for better results. So yes it will take some time to see some gains.

**Weight hanging** for penis enlargement usually involves the use of attaching device which grips on the glans of the penis, the weight will be suspended over a certain period of time on your penis and the motive behind the use of weight is to increase the weight on your penis. Be sure to be cautious using this method as you should only gently increase the weight you are comfortable with as to not tear any ligaments. You can achieve extensive penis growth by hanging penis enlargement weights for several weeks at 10-20 minutes per exercise.

## Supplements for Penis Enlargement

Penis enlargement pills, patches and drugs are often recommended for individuals who do not have much time for penis enlargement exercises or some other natural means of penis enlargements. Pills are quick an easy fix, which are better for sexual stamina not permanent enlargement of your penis. Size gains are only temporary. So you if you want lasting penis enlargement gains, yes you will have to take some time and dedication with exercises and using enlargement devices regularly to see significant improvement.

However keep dedicated to your penis regiment and you will see results!

The most recent and widely used penis supplement and pills comprises of two major amino acids- **L-Ornithine and L-Arginine**. These two amino acids are more common in supplements used by body builders to increase their bodies' endurances during physical activities and also speed up their recovery time. L-Argine is an amino acid produced naturally in the body, it is used in the making of penis enlargement pills because it plays a very vital role in the body's tissue and cardio-vascular health. L-arginine has been found to be capable of increasing the dilation of the blood vessels, ensuring that there is more inflow of blood in and out of the penis.

Another way through which an L-arginine supplement or pills can work for you is the substance that has been found to be capable of increasing the levels of Human Growth Hormone (HGH) in the body- this hormones help reduce stress by reducing fatigue, it is really helpful for you if your sexual dysfunction results from stress, fatigue and anxiety.

The usage of penis enlargement pills and supplements will depend on a number of factors, these include; health history of the user, the sexual life and pattern, age, and several others. A physician will ideally asked and investigate your medical history before recommending a particular penis enlargement pill or supplement for you, this will help you avoid some common problems and complications.

There are countless number of penis enlargement pills around, many of the low quality pills don't do much, you should not rely on online reviews only, contacting individuals who have actually used such pills in recent times may be your best possible way of detecting the authenticity of such products. "Hey buddy how are those penis pills working out for ya?"

## Medical/surgical penis enlargement

The most common medical procedure you can use to enlarge your penis size is Phalloplasty. This surgical procedure cannot be classified as a natural penis enlargement method because it is invasive in nature. I would highly recommend against going the surgical route. Aside the fact that surgical penis enlargement may cost you a lot of money, the invasive nature of such procedures can lead to a permanent damage to the tissues of your penis. In most cases surgical penis enlargement becomes painful and may require that an individual use analgesics.

Basically, the procedure of enlarging the penis through surgical means involve the surgeon cutting out the ligaments which hold the penis in position, and then your penis will be allowed to descend. With the use of a permanent surgical extender, your penis will be permanently elongated over a period of weeks. Performing a surgical penis enlargement on your penis will help you achieve between 1-2 inches of extra length and up to 1 inch of girth extension. Penis enlargement through surgery can leave you scars as well. Your erection will normally point downwards after the surgery and who wants that?

Dermal implant is another surgical technique through which your penis can be enlarged. Dermal implant involves the transplant of some fat cells from other parts of the body on to the penis. The head of the penis cannot be enlarged may make the whole process rather odd. Aside the fact that your penis head may look absurd with cells transfer, the accumulation of fat cells in a particular region of your penis may make your penis lumpy. The main reason why a surgeon may not perform this kind of surgical penis enlargement on you is because of the side effects.

If you are planning to perform a surgical penis enlargement procedure you should be ready to part with several thousands of dollars – usually between $2,000 - $5000 or more in some cases. In several cases, a surgical operator will ask for your health insurance cover before a surgical penis enlargement procedure is performed on you, the cost implications as well as a higher tendency to develop post surgical problems are the most common reasons why medical handlers ask.

If you can't afford a surgical penis enlargement operation, or you believe you wouldn't be able to handle the post operation problems, then your best bet is to make use of safer and less invasive natural penis enlargement methods without the high cost and side effects, and will give you long term penis enlargement.

## Problems with surgical operation for penis enlargement

The physical and psychological problems associated with surgical extension of the penis vary from mild to severe. Most surgical operations do come with complications. If you want to go for a surgical elongation of your penis, keep in mind that as many as 30% of those who go for surgical enlargement of penis do not feel completely satisfied with the result. Depending on the structure and nature of your penis growth, you should expect a minimum of 1 inch extension and most people do not achieve more than 2 inches. If you achieve less than 1 inch of penis growth through surgical operations, then there must be some underlying factors.

Post surgical operation infections and scarring may be witnessed during or after penis enlargement surgery. If you suffer from minor scars, such may heal over time but when such infection is turning to soreness or blisters, then you must consult your doctor for proper post-surgical operation treatment. Though your penis should heal in few days after the surgical operations, it may take several weeks in some cases. You may suffer from redness and itching while severe complications may include difficulty in urination, problems with erection and many others. You don't have to be scared of these complications as most of them will disappear in just a relatively short period of time.

Damages to surrounding tissues and nerves are also common. Some of the tissues surrounding the penis and those which take active part in the normal functioning of the penis may find it difficult to adjust to the new structure and size of the penis, in some cases they become damaged or malfunction.

There are several considerations that you must consider before choosing the ideal penis enlargement product and methods for yourself. You need to ensure that the safety of your penis as well as your general wellbeing is ensured. Most natural penis enlargement methods are safe to use, however getting the right concentration of usage or intensity will determine how safe you can use such methods and products.

You should consider the nature of your penis before deciding which enlargement product is ideal for you. If you suffer from erectile dysfunction, natural herbs might be the most suitable method for you, however if you are not suffering from any underlying health conditions such as erectile dysfunction, then you may go for mechanical devices. Treating underlying sexual conditions may be the first step towards choosing an ideal natural penis enlargement product for you.

Prices of natural penis enlargement products should have little effect on your choice of product, most herbal natural penis enlargement products come at cheaper prices compared to mechanical penis enlargement devices, though not all herbal products are cheaper than mechanical devices, this is one of the reasons why you should not allow prices of products to decide your choice of product. You should be careful of extremely cheap products that may be imitations of original products.

The best penis enlargement products should come with a limited warranty. This should include a full refund of money if the product does not cause a meaningful impact on your penis under a certain period of time. Some herbal product manufacturers will allow you to have a taste of what they have to offer for a limited period of time before you actually subscribe to buying the product package.

As per mechanical devices, it will be ideal for you to read product reviews online or ask individuals who have actually used such products to be able to determine which one that will work perfectly for you. The mechanical devices you choose must not be too fragile to break. Your mechanical device must not put any harm on your penis.

Penis enlargement pills and patches can be easily applied, but they must not trigger any form of allergic reaction. You should go for a natural penis supplements without additives. Generally be careful in your selection processes while choosing the ideal penis enlargement products for your needs. Be opened to advice from physicians, friends, and read as many reviews as possible.

# Part 2: 5 Natural and Easy-to-Find Ingredients for Boost Your Sex Life and Improve Sex Duration

## Chapter 1: Boosting Sex life

### Note Insecurities Down

Whenever you feel insecure about something, just write it down on a piece of paper. When you do this, you are going to make the insecurity something that you can objectively analyze. When you write your insecurity down, read it back to yourself. Question this insecurity, ask yourself why you feel this way. Is the insecurity valid? Is it necessary? Try to find out the source of this insecurity, and ask yourself if that source is even trustworthy.

Eventually you will start to see that a lot of your insecurities are the result of bad perceptions of yourself. You are not actually as bad as you make yourself out to be. However, your perception of yourself remains negative. It is this aspect of your life that you will truly be able to change once you start writing down your insecurities and analyzing them.

### Educate Yourself

There is a lot of shame that is commonly attributed to sex. What your preferences are, the way you feel about your body, a lot of these things are judged by people. You are made to feel unusual, a freak as it were. This is why it is so important to start educating yourself about sex. Learn about as many sexual preferences as possible. You will find out that a lot of your preferences are very commonplace. Even the most outlandish ones would be perfectly normal, with legitimate explanations. Unless you are a pedophile, it is highly unlikely that your sexual preferences will be so abhorrent that they would warrant disgust.

The fear of being judged plays a huge role in making men feel stressed out about sex. This stress usually results in erectile dysfunction more often than not.

## Do Things That Make you Feel the Way You Want to Feel

We live in exciting times. People no longer have to conform to enforced notions of gender anymore. A man is no longer less of a man if he cries, and he is no longer expected to be burly and stoic. You are, essentially, freer than ever before to be whoever you want to be. This means that a lot of your stress in not valid. Most men feel stressed out because they do not conform to these notions of masculinity. It is a natural occurrence, since this is the first generation that is emerging after those imposed notions of masculinity have been removed.

The best way you can build sexual confidence is being the kind of man you want to be. There are women and men out there with incredibly diverse tastes and preferences. This means that no matter what kind of man you want to be, you can be sure that there will be a host of potential partners for you. Stop worrying about being the "right" kind of man. There is no such thing. By worrying so much about something so meaningless, you are going to end up suffering from erectile dysfunction if you are not suffering from it already.

## Have More Sex

The only way you can get confident about sex is by having as much sex as possible. This might seem odd to you, but this really is the best way. If you are stressed out about sex, chances are your erectile dysfunction has not progressed to the point where you are completely unable to get erect. Even if you are, there are so many people in the world who would enjoy the kinkier side to sex that you can be sure that you would find someone willing to acquiesce to your requirements.

By having sex, you will realize that it really isn't that difficult. If you are young, there are plenty of opportunities to have sex. As long as you ensure that you are safe, having sex will help you develop a better body image as well. This is because having sex will instill in you the belief that you are not unattractive. After all, why would anyone have sex with someone unattractive?

## Remove the Negatives from your Vocabulary

Being self deprecating is fair, and can be funny in some occasions. However, this is only up to the point where it is amusing and not an actual representation of what you think about yourself. If you are constantly self deprecating, you are going to end up believing some of the things you are saying. Remain positive about your body image, and avoid all negative spaces where people would make you feel bad about yourself.

This is especially important for you as a man who is suffering from erectile dysfunction. If you are in a space where you feel as though you are being ridiculed or made to feel low about your dysfunction, leave that space immediately. The stress that would come from the ridicule will greatly exacerbate your erectile dysfunction.

## Look at Real Bodies

Watching porn and looking at male models might leave you with the impression that real men are ripped and muscular, and that they all have large penises. This is not the case at all. Real mean are fat and skinny, they are bald and hairy, and penis size ranges from four all the way to seven inches long. And each and every one of these men has sex. You can too, there is no reason why you are any less than any other man.

In order to form a better body image, try looking at as many real bodies as possible. Try going for amateur porn which would have normal men instead of studio porn where porn stars are chosen for their looks.

## Admit the Importance of Body Positivity

For a lot of people, body image issues is something only women suffer from. As a man, you can suffer from them too. Acknowledge this fact. Stressing out over your body image issues is probably what caused your erectile dysfunction in the first place, so try to acknowledge the importance of accepting your body.

## Turn on the switch

Variety is the spice of life, therefore to make yourself the desire of a woman; you must know how to spice things up, and how to explore various strategies to ensure that she receives maximum pleasure during sex.

On this note, we are going to discuss this chapter as a means to achieving two aims; the first aim is the tactical aim, that is a means to stay longer without ejaculation and the second is to be able to spice things up for maximum satisfaction.

When you are digging down your woman, always ensure that you are hitting the right note. How do I mean? Make sure that you are not the only one feeling the sensation, that your partner is also enjoying the rhythm. This could be easily known from her reaction during the sex. Though the reaction of a woman to the sensation of sex differs and it's dependent on the background and culture of the woman.

You can engage to have fun-filled time with your partner without untimely interruption from the flow of nature. I want to believe you do engage your woman with varieties of styles during sex, if not, you need to start doing it right away.

When you engage different styles, it makes you stay longer during sex. This is how it works; during the period of switching from one style to another, there is always a break when you either pause to assume another position or totally withdraw to be able to do different things from what you have been doing before. This serves as a means to ensure that you stay longer as the pressure is reduced on your penis during this short break.

At the same time, you also achieve the aim of making your woman enjoy sex with you the more because the pleasure a woman feels during sex is related to the angle at which she has been penetrated from. There are some positions you assume that put pressure on her G-spot, this kind of position makes her journey into the land of big-O very fast. For instance, when you enter your partner with her back on the ground and her two legs raised in the air in a missionary position, you are entering at an angle which gives you a hedge to be hitting the G-spot. This style is best practiced on the couch.

There are some styles you engage that put you at a vantage position to directly engage the clitoris. Doggy style is one of those styles that helps you to engage her clit; when you penetrate from the rear, you could use your hand to directly touch her clit intermittently during the penetration or in continuous fondling of her sensitive spot depending on her reaction to it, because the clit might get so sensitive during sex that it becomes painful when touched, you need to understand.

The degree to which your partner enjoys sex with you is determined by how creative you are in bed. To be more creative, you need to engage more styles during sex. At the same time, you need to be careful so you don't switch styles too often that it becomes absurd or make her feel uncomfortable. When you are engaging a style, wait to see her reaction towards the particular style, to be able to determine whether you should continue or switch. To know if she enjoys a particular style or not, you should have spent at least one to three minutes, then observe her response.

This is how you know the style you should continue or discontinue immediately, when you use a particular style and her moaning suddenly increase or you notice that she breathes faster at that point, that should send a signal to you that she is probably enjoying the position better. Then it is not the time to switch, you need to continue and even increase the pace if possible to be able to give her maximum satisfaction.

Meanwhile, you engage another position and her moaning suddenly decreases or even stop, or you begin to feel as if she is absent-minded during the engagement, it means she is bored by the position and not really enjoying it, then you might need to switch immediately.

Your switch must always be turned on during sex to maximize the game and make it optimum for your partner as the advantage is for the both of you. Naturally, some women enjoy a particular style better on bed, depending on their body structure. Some prefer the missionary position, to some; it is cow girl that does the job, to another it is doggy, while some prefer scissors, and others prefer 69 and so forth. There is nothing like "one size fit all" in the matter of sex position and styles, it varies from woman to woman.

Nonetheless, a survey was carried out among women of sexually active age, it was discovered that many women prefer doggy style based on their responses. It was also discovered that many women prefer to be in charge than to stay passive at the receiving end. Meaning that they want to be in control of the affairs during sex, cow girl, doggy and reverse cow girl are styles that fit such tendencies.

All these are opinion, the main job is to understand your woman and know what works best for her and how she loves to receive it.

SWITCH THE PACE

The switch is not only applied to your style, but also to your pace. It was discovered that your pace during sex also determines how much your partner will enjoy it. Oftentimes, the pace at which the penetration is done is dependent on the mood of the man or woman or even the environment. You will find out that when you are excited, your pace isn't slow like slot but fast and furious, and when you are not really in the mood, you just manage to go in and out slowly.

At some particular time, the environment tend to dictate the pace, maybe you are just stealing the show where a little noise will alert the next neighbor of what is going on, you tend to maintain a slow pace to save the situation. Unlike in a situation where you are as free as air, you just bang as fast as you can.

Reaction of women to pace also differs from woman to woman. Some prefer it slow and sexy, some want it fast and furious while others want to stay somewhere in the middle. That is why the point for you to know your woman cannot be overemphasized. Know your woman (KYW)

On a general note, I found out that majority of women prefer their mood to determine the pace during sex. Nevertheless, it was researched that fast paced sex achieves orgasm faster in women than the slow ones.

One of the merits of switching pace during sex is to help you control the time of ejaculation. For most men, fast pace means a quick ejaculation. Your pace also determines how long you will last in bed.

In order to control the duration of your sex, switch paces, alternate between fast and slow pace. You can start very slow, increase the pace as you proceed until you are really hitting it, maintain the tempo for a while, and then switch back to slow pace again as if in a cycle. By this practice, you will last longer on her than when you rush in with fast action and then rush out with cold feet.

As a matter of principle, don't always start penetrating with a fast pace, you could run out of energy; by the time she is already enjoying your fast rhythm, your body might start to feel as if it can't carry you any longer, your slow pace then will feel like a punishment to your woman. Therefore, start slowly and increase the momentum as you go. Practice it as if you are driving a car; increase the pace as you go.

# Chapter 2: How to improve sex duration

Many men are worried about their sexual performances. They want to last longer, to make their partners feel good, to be praised for their abilities. And it is nothing wrong with that. All people want to feel good, to enjoy themselves, to feel free and happy. But what do you really expect of your sexual performance? Do you want to satisfy your partner? Do you want to be better than last time? What is your goal? Sexual performance is not only about yourself; therefore "measuring" it can be more difficult, because you have to take into account multiple factors.

Who establishes your sexual performance? Is it you or your partner? Or both? You should answer these questions to know what you have to do. Usually, men define sexual performance as the time of the intercourse. The longer they last, the better they think everything is. And this is partially true. But time isn't everything. You can improve your performance in many ways, depending on the needs of your partner and your own expectations.

## First of all, you should try to relax.

Many men are obsessed with the idea of lasting longer. And, yes, women have to admit this is important, but is not everything. Other significant things are the attention for your partner, the physical touching, the connection between the two of you, the needs you and your partner have, the expectations you and your partner have. A good communication is the key to solving your sexual problems. If you can't talk to each other, if you don't know what your partner wants, you can't really improve your sexual performance.

## Try to focus on satisfying your partner.

This includes talking to her, finding out what she wants, what she needs, what she likes and dislikes. This should be your first step. Then, you can focus on lasting longer. There is some practical general advice you can follow to improve your sexual performance, like paying attention to your diet, exercising, reducing stress. In a short while, you will start seeing the difference.

The good news is that you can always improve your sexual performance, if you really want it. There is no age limit, you only have to know yourself and your partner. Yes, it is annoying and frustrating to experience erectile dysfunction, but this doesn't mean it is the end of your intimate life. Consider it is only a stepping stone you need to overcome.

If you know what you have to do, your sexual performance will increase and both your partner and you will be pleased about it. Here are some tips to improve your sexual performance:

Try to be relaxed. Stop thinking you will not make it and stop worrying about your erections. This puts an additional stress on your shoulders and it will end up affecting your erections. So, try to be relaxed, to enjoy the moments you can spend with your partner. Don't think at anything else, just live the moment and forget about anything else. Try to educate your mind to live in the present, without wondering here and there without a reason.

## Focus on cardiovascular exercise.

This improves your health and your sexual performance. You don't need to spend all day at the gym, thirty minutes a day are enough. Swimming and running are great methods to boost your libido and improve your erections. You can also practice other types of sports, depending on what you like. The most important thing is to exercise, to train your body and your mind, at the same time. This makes you feel healthy and be healthy.

Include in your diet the following: garlic, onion, bananas, chilies and peppers, omega-3 acids, eggs, vitamin B1. These contribute to your health and can significantly improve your sexual life.

Get some sun. This makes you feel better and is an excellent boost for your sexual desire. So don't stay inside, get out and enjoy your time. Fresh air is great for increasing your libido, especially summer days and nights. You can think of a vacation together with your partner in a hot destination, where you can practice every-thing you learn in this book.

Masturbation can help you last longer in bed. Before having sex with your partner, you can practice masturbation.

## Connect with your partner.

A great sexual experience involves the two of you. Therefore, don't focus only on your performance, because this will make your partner feel unimportant. Focus on making her feel relaxed, on do-ing the things she likes. As long as you are not constantly thinking on how to last longer, things will become better.

## See a sexologist.

This can be a very good way to learn more about yourself, your sexuality and what you can do to improve your intimate life. You can bring your partner with you and discuss about your problems and your expectations. There is nothing to feel ashamed about. Imagine, these people have to do this every day and they probably heard many things during their careers. So try to be honest and see this experience as an opportunity to find out new things and resolve your problems.

## Try new things.

Routine is the enemy of a great sexual life, so do the best you can to avoid it. Try changing the place, the way you dress, try role-playing, whatever keeps you away from routine. Talk to your partner about what you should improve and do the best you can to come to an agreement. A relationship needs time and communication; is not something you can easily do or understand.

## Increase your self-confidence.

Usually, women are more likely to have low self-confidence, but this can also happen to men. If you don't trust yourself, if you are thinking on how to last longer and can't get relaxed, you will only make things worse. To increase your self-confidence, try to adopt a positive attitude; do something for yourself, like buying a nice jacket or a new perfume, cut your hair in a different way. See what makes you feel good about yourself, because this will also increase your self-confidence and improve your sexual performance.

## Try different positions.

In order to avoid routine and discover new ways of enjoying your intimate life, you should try new positions. Talk to your partner about her fantasies, about what she would like to try, tell her about your own fantasies and try new things. Establish a line you are not allowed to cross, according to your wishes.

## Practice Kegel exercises.

They have many benefits and can be practiced by both men and women. You can do them anywhere, at home, while driving, while cooking, at your office or anywhere else. Tighten your pelvic muscle and keep the contraction for a couple of seconds before releasing. You should repeat at least 10 times for a set and you can do multiple sets every day. In time, this improves your erections and makes you able to control yourself for a longer period of time.

## Be patient.

If you are going through a difficult time at work, give yourself the time to overcome the problem. Don't expect things to solve immediately and don't become a pessimistic. Instead, try to focus on finding a solution for your problem, without blaming yourself. Even if you decide to see a doctor, don't expect things to change within a week. It takes time to find out what is going wrong, what you should do and it is important to know you can count on the support of your partner.

## Never give up.

Sometimes, it takes time to discover the cause of erectile dysfunction and this can be quite frustrating. You may need to try several treatments, but you should not give up. It is only a matter of time and will to succeed. Trial and error is sometimes inevitable, if you aren't lucky enough to get the perfect treatment from the very first time.

You can try supplements or special food to increase your libido, but only with the doctor's recommendation. Don't take supplements without consulting a doctor, because they can have many side effects and interfere with other medication you are taking. They can affect your heart and the well-functioning of your body. As much as you would like to believe they are the answer to your problems, this is rarely the case. Don't play games with your health. If you want to avoid this, always see a doctor before taking supplements.

## Stay focused

A major bane of poor performance among men from the perspective of the women is self-centered sex. Sex could be self-centered especially from men, it is surprising how some men set examination by themselves, score the script and organize an award ceremony for themselves. This is true about guys who boast of how great they are in bed without realizing that the performance is only being endured by the partner.

Great sex is not defined from one angle alone. You can't say you are good in bed because you do enjoy the feelings. The question is; does your partner enjoy the act, or she is just trying to get along so that your ego will not be affected? Great sex is measured by how satisfied are the parties involved, did you both enjoy the ride? If you are given a chance in the next few hours, will you love to have same kind of feeling again?

This is one of the secrets of becoming the desire of a woman. The way you love to enjoy the sweet sensation of orgasm is the exact way a woman wants to enjoy it too, if not more. Most men concentrate on themselves and their attention is only on the time they will ejaculate.

If you can have a paradigm shift from this moment and ensure that every sexual encounter with your partner will be all about her, you will see how she will begin to desire the time with you.

A client shared with me on how his wife does not like to go down with him in bed. He concluded that his wife hates sex because she refuses most of his sexual advances. It became a tension in their home and the marriage was almost falling apart. When I interviewed the man about how long he desires to have sex with his wife, his response indicated that he wants sex almost every day or if possible twice a day. I further probed him about how many times at least in a week does his wife reach climax during sex, from his response, he was not sure if the wife has ever experienced orgasm in their marriage. I was not surprised by this response because many women above the age of forty are yet to experience orgasm for once according to a survey.

If you are in the class of men who engage in self-centered sexual intercourse, you need to stop it now. Such an act is counterproductive.

Sex should bring about mutual pleasure to the people involved; it should not be a one-sided thing. Many a times, the women are free from this guilt of self-centeredness in sex even though we have some women who are also self-centered in bed, but it is more pronounced among men because the point of orgasm of a man is easy to come by unlike that of woman who requires constant efforts, skills and experience.

As a man, how good you are in bed is determined by how good she feels during each encounter with you. Having realized this, you need to learn how to always make her feel good during sex with you. Please, don't put yourself under pressure as pressure itself has a way of sabotaging your effort and make it counterproductive. The key is for you to keep getting better every day until you become a 'pro'.

Can you imagine your partner getting to orgasm at every encounter? It will tell on her general outlook as we will be happier than those who hardly experience orgasm. It makes your partner look younger and it gives freshness to her skin. The glow on her face alone after sex and the big smile that follows is enough to convince you to always desire to make her climax at every encounter.

A major factor in becoming the desire of your woman is to focus the attention on her pleasure, let her enjoyment become your priority. Have sex as if you have no stake in it, let your attention be on her, be determined to always make your partner enjoy sex. As you think about sex, think of her interest first and how you can take her to the climax where she will like to be ever time.

Just as I explained in the past chapter about how sex starts from the mind of a woman, engage her mind to focus on sex for the moment. For example, during your normal discussion, you could just bring up some erotic conversation and ask of her opinion. Sex might be the least on her mind at that moment, but this will make her begin to think of sex and probably begin to prepare her mind to enjoy sex with you. Research has it that an average man thinks about sex nineteen times a day while an average woman thinks about sex ten times a day. That is why as a man, you should have a way of preparing her for sex.

Having done that, when the time comes for the real deal; take it slowly. Be gentle, polite and caring. You might be wondering why I am detailing the process; from experience, I have learnt that many men are very clumsy in bed; they rush the entire process and lose the very reason for the act. Therefore, one cannot over emphasize the point that you need to take time to enjoy the entire process each time you want to get down with your woman.

It is good to start with pillow talk, the heart to heart discussion that reveals things that are bugging her mind, it may be stress from her place of work or the children's health or whatever, the heart to heart discussion will help free her mind from the stress and worries to be able to concentrate on the pleasure of the moment. Note that if this process is skipped and she still has things bothering her, it might hinder her ability to climax. When sex is performed with an open mind, it enhances her ability to cum quickly.

After the discussion, move to foreplay and continue from there, as discussed in a previous chapter.

Great sex is a possibility, channel your energy towards giving her pleasure and she will want to be with you every moment of her life and you will also observe that she's becoming more protective of you, she won't want any other woman share from the kind of pleasure she is receiving. That's the beauty of becoming an action man.

# Chapter 3: Ingredients to boost sex life and duration

Since a big chunk of erectile dysfunction is physiological, it stands to follow that good nutrition is key to addressing the issue. Great nutrition is all about wise eating habits and choices. Unfortunately, it isn't always possible to get all the necessary nutrients by simply eating the right foods. Often times, supplementation is needed. Eating right for addressing or reducing the risks for erectile dysfunction may require taking supplements for optimal penile health. Truth is, natural supplements, e.g., herbs, have been used since time immemorial in addressing erectile issues by African and Chinese cultures.

Compared to prescription medications for treating erectile dysfunctions such as Cialis (tadalafil), Levitra (vardenafil) and Viagra (sildenafil), supplements don't have as extensive studies or tests to back up their efficacy claims. As the amount and type of active ingredients among different erectile dysfunction supplements may vary, their side effects do so as well.

Because supplementation can be quite helpful to address erectile dysfunctions, here's a guide for choosing erectile dysfunction supplements:

Generally safe, with positive results from studies of people

➤ DHEA: There's some amount of evidence showing its ability to address erectile dysfunction. Generally safe at low doses but have been reported to cause acne in some cases.

➤ L-ARGININE: There's some evidence establishing its ability to stimulate wider blood vessel opening to increase blood flow. In some cases, it's been reported to cause diarrhea, cramps and nausea. Avoid taking together with Viagra.

➤ GINSENG: Panax ginseng has been shown in one study to improve sexual function for men who suffer from erectile dysfunction. It's cream form – applied topically – can help prevent premature ejaculation. Although generally safe for short-term use, using panax ginseng as a supplement can cause insomnia for some people.

With positive results from studies of people but higher risk

➤ YOHIMBE: Some clinical studies have shown yohimbe to help improve erectile dysfunctions brought about by anti-depressant medications but have also been reported to cause relatively serious side effects in some people like anxiety, irregular heartbeat and elevated blood pressure. As such, this supplement should only be taken with approval from a licensed physician.

No significant studies on people

➤    GINGKO: This herbal supplement has good potential to improve penile blood flow but no solid evidence exists regarding claims of effectively addressing erectile dysfunction. A potential side effect of this herbal supplement is risk for bleeding.

➤    HORNY GOAT WEED (EPIMEDIUM): Although the leaves of this herb contain ingredients that are used for better sexual performance, there are no established studies on people that support the belief in its efficacy. A bonus side effect of this herbal supplement is it can help lower blood pressure.

Other non-prescription herbal alternatives

Several herbal products that claim to be the "natural" Viagra proliferate the market. The thing is, these products have undisclosed quantities of potent ingredients that are also found in their supposed synthetic counterparts and thus have higher risks for un-wanted side effects. In fact, some of these products actually con-tain the very drugs that their supposed synthetic counterparts have that require a doctor's prescription to consume! In this case, it's best to be very vigilant in taking "herbal" erectile dysfunction supplements from manufacturers that aren't well known or don't have a good reputation in the market. Even if the FDA has banned such "herbal" supplements, they continue to proliferate illegally.

Remember, it's not enough that manufacturers claim that theirs are herbal – it's easy to claim such stuff without backing them up. Because it's practically impossible for ordinary consumers like you and I to distinguish, it's best to stick with relatively more ex-pensive brands of herbal supplements from well-established man-ufacturers.

Being labeled "herbal" doesn't necessarily mean safe. Remember, they may be say taken as is but some of them may react negatively if taken with other medications. As such, it's best to consult with a licensed physician first prior to taking such supplements for erectile dysfunction, especially when taking regular medications.

Online purchase risks

With the proliferation of many online stores these days and the convenience shopping on such stores brings, no wonder many people choose to buy their supplements online. Beware though – many supplements for erectile dysfunction that are sold online these days contain ingredients that need prescription or worse, are undisclosed.

Many men who purchase erectile dysfunction supplements online think these are safe because of the nice packaging. These are often labeled as "all-natural" or "safer than prescription medicines but are just as effective." The scary truth is often times, the label tells a different story than the content. The worse thing that can happen is that these supplements contain dangerous ingredients that aren't on the label. In fact, the United States Food And Drugs Administration (FDA) – through its Internet and Health Fraud division – conducted an online survey that revealed more than 1/3 of erectile dysfunction supplements purchased online contained prescription grade ingredients and other similar substances that weren't even disclosed.

Two of these are the ingredients sildenafil and vardenafil (or substances very similar to these), the active ingredients for Viagra and Levitra, respectively. If people who have issues with Viagra and Levitra take these supplements thinking they're safer than the two prescription medicines, they may be in for a rude awakening as they suffer from side effects that they're trying to avoid in the first place.

What's more, even if the men taking these supplements have no issues with Viagra or Levitra, it's possible for them to suffer adverse side effects if they're taking medicines that don't mix well with the 2 prescription medicines' active ingredients that aren't disclosed in the supplements. For example, if a person is taking prescription medicine that contains nitrates, taking supplements that unknowingly contain sildenafil (an active component of Viagra) may bring down his blood pressure dangerously low. Nitrates are a common ingredient in prescription medicines used to treat or manage heart disease, high cholesterol, high blood pressure and diabetes and incidentally, men who are being treated for these conditions also suffer from erectile dysfunction.

**Non-oral solutions for erectile dysfunction**

Until recently, medical or supplemental treatments for erectile dysfunction were taken orally. Although those may work well for many, there are some men who aren't predisposed to the ingredients of such medicines or supplements, especially those who take prescription medicines that contain nitrates. Oral treatments may also have side effects that can negate the erection benefits offered.

Now, non-oral treatments are available for erectile dysfunctions as an alternative to oral treatments. They vary in efficacy and side effects. To help you sift through them, here's a list of the most popular topical solutions for erectile dysfunction:

➤    AndroGel: Many cases of erectile dysfunctions are caused by low testosterone levels. One of the most popular ways of addressing this deficiency is testosterone replacement but technically, it doesn't help men with normal levels of testosterone and those who suffer from erectile dysfunction. Testosterone can also be delivered by skin application via AndroGel – testosterone in a gel. Some of the potential side effects worth noting are emotional instability, acne and headache.

➤    Alprostadil: This kind of topical solution is classified as a vasodilator, substances that can help blood vessels to expand and improve blood flow. Since erectile dysfunction is physically a blood flow issue, Alprostadil is used for treating erectile dysfunction and is administered directly via injection into the penis or suppository insertion into the urethra. In has a reported efficacy rate of about 80%. There are no known side effects.

Alprostadil is also available as a topically applied solution, which spares men from penile scarring, bleeding and bruising. Tests have confirmed that it helps in most erectile dysfunction cases with minimal and tolerable side effects.

# Chapter 4: Nutririon for Penis Enlargement

Supplements can be ingested in numerous structures, either through pills or supplements, entire sustenances, teas, herbs, and so forth... It is essential to illuminate that supplements alone will never for all time enlarge your penis. Be that as it may, appropriate supplementation can extraordinarily AFFECT THE RATE OF PENIS GROWTH while executing a penis enlargement schedule.

These 8 components are the basic variables in amplifying the impacts of a penis enlargement schedule. They can each be actuated through different means utilizing a portion of the supplements we have recorded underneath.

The response to this is troublesome, and the reason is straightforward. For the sake of science, we can not ensure that a supplement will give the fancied impacts, unless it is clinically demonstrated. The procedure of clinically demonstrating something to work, particularly in the realm of nourishment, is extremely troublesome for some reasons. All things considered, on the grounds that something has no 'logical approval', does not imply that it is not successful.

Many supplements are guaranteed to have the wanted impacts that improve penis enlargement. Luckily some of them really have investigative backing, yet numerous don't. On this site we break down whatever number of these supplements as could be expected under the circumstances and give you our legitimate knowledge on every one. The following is a rundown of all supplements that have been found in several penis enlargement or male upgrade supplements.

Eating appropriately has numerous huge medical advantages, including noteworthy penis enlargement advantages. The accompanying penis enlargement sustenances can offer you some assistance with getting the additional bigness and length size you have been longing for. Also, not at all like over-the-counter penis enlargement tranquilizes, these penis enlargement nourishments are sheltered, shabby, and sound.

You will know more need to stress over unsafe substances, unnerving symptoms, and paying a fortune. Furthermore, if that wasn't already enough, we tossed in our suggested penis enlargement vitamins too! Do you know of any penis enlargement nourishments that we disregarded? Tell us in the remark area beneath!

## Lifestyle For Your Penis

Writing about a healthy lifestyle alone can fill several books. Therefore, I can only give a brief overview of how your lifestyle affects the erection or the size of your penis. But you will have realized it by now and it's hardly surprising: the way you live, will have an impact on your penis! Just in case you are already feeling resistance when reading these lines, because you do not want to give up cherished practices, that is of course fine. Nonetheless, remind yourself quickly, what pleasures you can gain through all of that! Even if a higher life expectancy alone is not a cause for change, maybe you will be convinced by great sex and larger sex stamina until old age?

## 1. **Smoking**:

Smoking is not only harmful to your overall health, but endangers your penis as well - at least its growth in size and its ability to have erections. **Because smoking decreases the blood flow**! This is also the very reason why smokers often have cold hands. And you do know what happens when there is low blood flow in your penis, right?!

## 2. **Stress**:

Stress is the cause of many diseases and the No. 1 cause of death in the United States. Therefore, it makes sense to reduce or avoid stress in your life wherever it is possible. Similarly, if you have ever tried to have sex when you were under tremendous stress, then you know what I mean. You may want it a lot, and stand across from the most beautiful woman, but still your body is not cooperating. The result: Your penis is limp. Embarrassing as this is, it is also, unnecessary. Because stress is avoidable, becaus we allow us to be stressed through other people, bad time management, wrong priorities, etc. But for the benefits of your cock, start making different decisions to improve things on a basic level.

## 3. **Sleep**:

Let me say this clearly: too little sleep can be absolutely devastating for your sex life! If you are so tired that you cannot think straight, your penis is guaranteed to not be in top form. If you can barely stand up straight from sheer weariness, how should your cock do it successfully then? And let's just assume that it somehow pulls itself together - just for you – obviously there will be no peak performance. So, if you prefer your erections to be rock hard and to remain like that, ensure adequate sleep.

## 4. **Mindset**:

Do you want a long, thick, rock hard cock permanently? I'll tell you how to get it...

**It's simple: you have to believe that it works!** Stop with all the self-doubt. Stop the inner critic who bullies you at every opportunity (and laughs at your penis). Once you believe in your success, take concrete actions and stick to it until you have reached your goal, then you will inevitably have success.

THE PICK UP BIBLE WITH TIPS AND TRICKS [2 IN 1] BY LIL REY

And there is an extra bonus on top of it all: Did you know that you will automatically increase your self-confidence by doing so? And this special boost in confidence it not due to the increased size of your cock.

Because the more consistent you are doing something with self-discipline, the more confident you become. You can start relying on yourself. And isn't this great?

## 5. **Fitness**:

The proper strength training makes you manly and releases testosterone. You can support the penis exercise with it, provided it is intense enough to stimulate the natural production of testosterone and muscle growth. Pick an exercise program where you are working with heavier weights and small number of repetitions. Very deliberate and slow exercises are particularly effective at promoting testosterone production, because they provide good muscle build up.

## 6. **Diet**:

If you want faster or better results, this is THE alternative for you! Eat the right foods and spice up your diet with additional matching supplements of purely natural origin and your progress will accelerate tremendously. In so doing significantly more growth is possible - in a safe and healthy manner. This way the blood will be enriched with all the improved nutrient supply, which promotes rapid growth.

If you do now the exercises described here, the chemically enriched blood will flow increasingly into the penis, and all those substances will be made available and encourage your penis to grow and become larger. The longer you can keep up the erection then, the more you will benefit from the high-quality nutrients, with which the blood is enriched.

## Measure, But Do it Correctly

**Do not overdo it!**

Let me repeat it here again: Please, do not overdo it with the exercises. Impatience gives you nothing but harm! Stay persistent and do the exercises regularly. Then you will succeed and see significant progress.

Do you really want to up the ante and accelerate your penis growth and give it more inches? Then there is only one way to do it that is effective and safe: Change your diet! Because, as already mentioned, an increased supply of nutrients accelerates the growth process. And that is the only sensible, safe and healthy way to speed things up.

**Regular Measurements**

a. **Do not measure daily**: Of course you are interested in how much progress is achieved, and if your dick has finally become longer, but still, do not measure it every day! Because, even if you gain, for example, 8 mm in 2 months, this corresponds to a growth of only 0.13 mm per day. It is impossible to measure these small daily increases.

b. **Exactly defined intervals**: Select a specific time interval, for example, every 3-4 weeks where you regularly measure. Would you like to do it even better? Take on that day 3 different measurements and calculate the average. In this way, you compensate for fluctuations, because no man has always the same erection!

c. **Always measure in the same way**: This is actually the most important thing, because then you minimize measurement errors.

Always measure in the same position (sitting, standing or lying down)

Always use the same ruler (no set square, or a ruler that rolls up)

Make sure to always get the same angle of the penis to the ground

Last but not least: Learn to measure correctly!

**Various measurement methods**

**BPEL - Bone Pressed Erect Length**: This method is relatively accurate, and is, therefore, most frequently used. Once you have reached full erection, take the ruler and press it over the base of the penis directly against the abdomen on to the pelvic bone. Therefore the name "Bone Pressed".

**NBPEL - None Bone Pressed Erect Length**: Only the visible, erect penis length is measured, which begins outside the skin. Unlike BPEL, do not force the ruler against the pelvic bone, but put it down only slightly on the abdomen. **(This method is more inaccurate.)**

**BPFL - Bone Pressed Flaccid Length**: Here the penis is measured in the soft state. As with the BPEL also, place the ruler at the base of the penis and press it against the pelvic bone. However, it is often difficult to measure the penis size when flaccid, because many factors can affect the penis! Think only of the cold water in the swimming pool. **(This method is also more inaccurate.)**

**BPFSL - Bone Pressed Flaccid Stretched Length**: The penis is flaccid. You put the ruler right next to the base of the penis, and press it against the abdomen or pelvic bone. Then, pull on the penis until it reaches its maximum length. In this way, you "simulate" the erect length of the penis. Usually, the thus measured length corresponds surprisingly accurately to the actual erect penis length. It is a relatively safe indication that the penis enlargement exercises work, if this measuring method shows a change. In this way, progress can most immediately be recognized, even if the actual growth in the erect penis can often only be seen a little later.

**EG - Erect Girth**: This way, you measure the girth of your penis. For that, you just put a tape measure around the erect penis and measure either at the base of the penis, in the middle or just below the glans! Always measure at the same place.

**Penis diameter**: If you want the exact diameter of your penis, use the following formula: diameter = circumference / Pi (Pi is 3.1415). If you now have a penis circumference of 10 cm, the diameter of your penis: 3.18 cm (10 cm /3.1415)

# Conclusion

Wherever you are standing at this moment, you are holding in your hands, a working system, with which you too can train your penis up to your desired size. The techniques presented herein are proven to work and have helped thousands of men grow their penis by several inches - in extreme cases to even grow up to 4 inches.

But there is a price to pay: you have to work for it and you need patience with yourself. Because, the growth phase of every man is different! So don't look for immediate results, go for the long term gain. You CAN do it too!

Also is a harder training not necessarily better, but can be dangerous. You are responsible for your health. These exercises are very safe, if they are properly applied. Stop immediately, if you feel any discomfort or perhaps even pain during an exercise, and increase the intensity slowly!

In addition to the aforementioned techniques, you have learned other factors that influence the growth of your penis. And if you take all the teachings and exercises seriously and keep at it, the reward is not only an impressive penis, but a rock hard erection and a better sex! In front of you lies a truly happy sex life, with a penis of which, up to now, you have only dreamt of!

All the best!